AD

Reimagining ~~workplace Well-Being~~

The workplace has incredible potential to provide opportunities for meaningful work, more enriching and supportive relationships, and moments of joy and creativity. A delightful mix of research, compelling stories, and practical insights, *Reimagining Workplace Well-Being* inspires a new way of addressing the heart and soul of employee well-being.

—**CHIP CONLEY,** MBA
Founder, Modern Elder Academy
Author of *Wisdom at Work*

Substantial research demonstrates the power of tapping into our purpose and values to help us make healthier choices and to live more meaningful, fulfilling lives. Yet how to implement this important science has remained elusive. *Reimagining Workplace Well-Being* describes this new research in easy-to-understand ways and shows us how to apply it in creating more holistic and pragmatic employee well-being approaches. Through science-backed insights, organizational case studies, and her own journey from burnout to thriving, Dr. Grossmeier keeps our minds engaged while also moving our hearts. Her groundbreaking and practical approach is one that even the most innovative organizations will want to know about and put to use.

—**MICHELLE SEGAR,** PhD, MPH
University of Michigan sustainable-behavior-change researcher
Author of *The Joy Choice* and *No Sweat!*

Reimagining Workplace Well-Being is a practical book providing clear guidance for employers looking to address the core elements of human thriving. Dr. Grossmeier is one of the best in the entire field when it comes to understanding the cutting edge while also staying grounded in scientific research and citing real-world examples that demonstrate how leading employers are translating this research into practice.

—**NEWTON CHENG,** MBA
Director, Global Health and Performance at Google

As we navigate an existential time, people crave more meaning, more purpose, and more connection. In *Reimagining Workplace Well-Being*, Dr. Grossmeier demystifies these core elements of spiritual well-being, makes an evidence-based argument for why a roadmap toward transcendence is needed more than ever and provides a practical framework to elevate these deep human needs in every workplace.

—LAURA PUTNAM, MA
CEO of Motion Infusion
Author of *Workplace Wellness That Works*

A tour de force, this book covers ground not represented in one place. *Reimagining Workplace Well-Being* brilliantly merges Dr. Grossmeier's deep knowledge of the workplace well-being field with the possibilities extant in the workplace spirituality field. I especially appreciate her role modeling of vulnerability and authenticity, with so much of her heart and soul accessible on page after page.

—PAUL TERRY, PhD
Senior Fellow, Health Enhancement Research Organization
Editor of the *American Journal of Health Promotion*

Reimagining Workplace Well-Being helps us move beyond check-the-box wellness programs by addressing the heart and soul of employee well-being. While heavily steeped in research, Dr. Grossmeier's sharing of the peaks and valleys in her own professional journey kept me engaged. It is a refreshingly vulnerable and authentic discussion that inspires us to consider how we might create a fulfilling workplace culture that truly invites employees to commit their best selves to their work.

—KENNETH R. PELLETIER, PhD, MD
Clinical Professor of Medicine
Author of *Change Your Genes, Change Your Life*

Spirituality has always been an essential dimension of human thriving, but many organizations have been reluctant to address it in their approach to employee well-being. Dr. Grossmeier's book shines a light on the robust evidence supporting a more holistic approach to workplace well-being. As a previous collaborator and ongoing mentor, I can attest to Jessica's discipline in walking her talk and appreciate her candor as she shares the role of spirituality in contributing to her own growth and development as a researcher and thought leader.

—**JACK GROPPEL,** PhD
Co-founder, Johnson & Johnson Human Performance Institute
Author of *The Corporate Athlete*

There is beauty and inspiration when we lay aside our differences to pursue a grander vision of something so audacious we dare not seek it on our own. *Reimagining Workplace Well-Being* clearly articulates the contributions that purpose, deep connection, and transcendence have on our individual and collective well-being. I recommend it to leaders who know the old way is broken. I recommend it to leaders who know deep down that just about every aspect of their organization, strategy, and culture must evolve for individuals and organizations to thrive.

—**BRANDON PEELE,** MBA
CEO of Unity Lab
Author of *Purpose Work Nation*

Reimagining Workplace Well-Being inspires leaders and wellness professionals to include workplace spirituality in their approach to advancing health and well-being. As someone who has worked with hundreds of leaders at all levels across numerous global corporations, I can attest to the value of incorporating the elements recommended in the book into efforts to develop leaders, teams, and work cultures. *Reimagining Workplace Well-Being* is a terrific resource for anyone in a position of leadership, whether an individual contributor, a team manager, or an organization executive.

—**RENEE MOOREFIELD,** PhD
CEO, Wisdom Works Group

REIMAGINING
WORKPLACE
WELL-BEING

Fostering a Culture of Purpose, Connection, and Transcendence

JESSICA GROSSMEIER, PhD, MPH

modern wisdom
PRESS

modern wisdom
P R E S S

Modern Wisdom Press
Boulder, Colorado, USA
www.modernwisdompress.com

Published 2022
Cover Design: Karen Sperry Design
Author photo courtesy of Christopher J. Grossmeier

ISBN: 978-1-951692-19-3 (paperback), 978-1-951692-20-9 (epub)

To my husband and best friend, Chris.
Your pushback challenges me and keeps me sharp.
Your support and love made this book possible.

AND

To the One who is able to do abundantly more than all we ask or imagine,
according to the power that works within us.

Contents

Getting to Why

by Victor J. Strecher, PhD, MPH

Faced with his own early mortality, Marshall Becker, one of the founders in the field of health behavior, wrote, "The purpose of life is not only to be happy; it is to matter—to be productive, to be dedicated to goals higher than one's own self-indulgence; in other words, to have it make some difference to the world that you have lived at all." Can we better understand and harness this transcendent mindset to create a new direction in workplace well-being? I believe we can, and Jessica Grossmeier's new book shows us the way to do it. And we need to do it.

In an earlier piece entitled "The Tyranny of Health Promotion," Becker wrote, "I feel certain that, when Socrates said 'The life which is unexamined is not worth living,' he was not thinking of individuals filling out Health Risk Appraisals." He is, as Jessica does in this book, encouraging us to examine our lives, to examine the "why" at least as much as the "how" of our lives. Because, to paraphrase Aristotle (the philosophical grandchild of Socrates), the unexamined life is not worth living, but the purposeless life isn't worth examining in the first place.

It's taken a while for the wellness industry to catch up with these philosophers from 2,400 years ago. In fact, traditional "eat, move, sleep" workplace wellness programming, often prefaced with a Health Risk Appraisal, still has not. Employees enrolled in these programs often feel they've heard the same admonishments and read the same "how to" material a million times. Randomized trials of these traditional programs have not been promising from a behavior change, a health improvement, or a cost savings perspective.

Despite continued use of these programs in the commercial world, researchers have understood the reasons for their failure for nearly two decades. They've also, through nearly thousands of studies, been discovering more promising directions. Therapeutic approaches including Motivational Interviewing, Acceptance and Commitment Therapy, and theories such as Self-Determination Theory and Self-Affirmation Theory have demonstrated impressive outcomes. Why? Because of their focus on the "why."

One explicit "why" of traditional wellness programs is to live a long life. Health Risk Appraisal, a mainstay of the traditional wellness industry, focuses on this outcome, typically providing a "risk age" or "real age" compared with one's chronologic age, and it supplies ways to live a longer life. In our own research and that of others, this approach does not appreciably motivate change.

In fact, sometimes the *acceptance* of one's mortality becomes a motivator for deeper awareness and exploration of how to spend one's time while on this planet. And this exploration leads us to the question of purpose.

This approach to living can be deeply motivating. Dedication, as Becker says, "to goals higher than one's own self-indulgence" requires energy, our most valuable resource, which in turn requires attention to our behaviors and mindset. We're no longer simply trying to be happy through a series of hedonic pleasures or trying to live forever. We're striving to become, as Jonas Salk stated, "good ancestors." Traditional workplace wellness programs typically fail to even understand much less address this root cause of lasting change.

Jessica addresses these seemingly lofty issues directly, carefully, and *practically*. This is a book for practitioners, and it clearly lays out the steps for a new generation of well-being programming. The book places our deepest motivators, purpose and connection, at the core of well-being. Through neural, behavioral, and epigenetic sciences, the concepts of purpose and connection are given a clear connection to physical parts and processes of the human body. This isn't new-age babble. This is science.

Why focus on these essential needs in the workplace? First, the easy responses: Most adults in the United States spend most of their waking hours working. The workplace can be a channel for engagement and support of behaviors considered mutually beneficial to the employee and employer. Moreover, the type of work and how it's performed is associated with health and well-being outcomes.

Perhaps more important, however, is that work itself can provide connection, joy, and, yes, fulfillment of one's purpose. As Studs Terkel states in his book *Working*, "Work is about the search, too, for daily meaning as well as daily bread, for recognition as well as for cash, for astonishment rather than torpor; in short, for a sort of life rather than a Monday through Friday sort of dying."

A few months ago, the president of a major corporation sent me a request for employee interventions that are ". . . on the intersection of mental wellness, human capital management, and employee benefits." Purpose and connection not only motivate well-being outcomes, they're also strongly associated with human capital management goals of work engagement and retention. This is because teams and organizations can also have purpose. Show me a sports team that lacks shared purpose and connection, and I'll show you a losing season.

In this book, Jessica revives lessons learned over 2,400 years ago, now supported by the most modern scientific evidence. Helping employees live big lives, meaning transcendent, purposeful lives in connection with others, is, I believe, an important mission of the next generation of wellness programming.

This book shows us how it can be done.

Vic Strecher is a professor at the University of Michigan's School of Public Health and Director for Innovation and Social Entrepreneurship. He authored the book **Life on Purpose** *and the graphic novel* **On Purpose***. He is the founder and Chief Purpose Officer at Kumanu, a company devoted to helping people identify and live out their purpose in everyday life.*

The Heart and Soul of Workplace Well-Being

"We can't fully optimize our well-being,
we can't understand how to build a foundation for good health,
if we don't understand the interplay between our mental health,
our physical health, and our spiritual health."

— VIVEK MURTHY

My Wake-Up Call

What have I done? I am lying on the cold wood floor in my bathrobe with my eyes closed, feeling as if someone has hit the side of my face with a hammer. I hear my husband, Chris, talking to someone on the telephone and strain to focus on what he is saying.

"I'm not sure what happened. I heard a loud sound like something falling on the floor. I was asleep and the sound woke me up. At first, I thought that maybe one of our cats knocked something on the floor. I called out to my wife when I noticed she wasn't in bed, and she didn't answer me. I got up and went into the living room to see what had happened and saw my wife lying face down on the floor. I turned her over onto her back and she wasn't breathing. I opened her mouth to administer rescue

1

breathing like I learned in my CPR classes, and she coughed up blood and then started to breathe on her own. But she still isn't responding to me, and I think she might be unconscious."

Wait just a minute. I fell? I wasn't breathing? I'm unconscious? I coughed up blood?! I open my eyes and see Chris crouched over me with his phone in his hand. He's giving someone our street address. Then he sees my eyes open and calls out to me, "Jess! Can you hear me? If you can, don't move, just blink your eyes a couple of times."

I blink my eyes to let him know that I hear him, and he exclaims into the phone, "She's conscious! She just opened her eyes and blinked a couple of times when I asked her to." He looks into my eyes and says, "Don't move, you fell." Then he directs his attention back to his conversation on the phone, appearing to be listening to instructions. I take a few deep breaths through my nose and try to make sense out of my circumstances. The last thing I remember was that I was about to get into the shower and that I felt dizzy. I lay back down in bed for a moment, trying to figure out what to do. I had a plane to catch for a business trip and if I lay in bed too long, I would miss my flight. I thought that maybe I was hungry and decided to go to the kitchen for a banana. Then, nothing. *What happened?*

Chris wraps up the call with the paramedics, and I ask him why he called 911 and why I'm lying in the middle of the living room floor. He explains he isn't sure what happened, but it seems I must have fallen and might have broken my jaw because my chin was set in a strange position when he turned me over. I may need stitches and might have broken a tooth or something because my gums are bleeding.

He asks me, "Do you have any idea why you fell? Did you trip over the cat or something?" I tell him that I was dizzy when I got up to shower and decided to get a banana and lay down on the sofa. Apparently,

I never made it to the kitchen. It's a story I repeat several times over the course of the day as I make my way through a labyrinth of health care professionals from the admitting nurse at the emergency room to the ER physician who gives me stitches to the X-ray technician to the resident specialist who confirms I broke my jaw by the fall. The only consolation during the entire day is when the specialist recommends I not have surgery to get my jaw wired shut because so many nerves intersect where the break is. She suggests that because I only broke the jaw in one place, the bone could mend on its own without having to immobilize it artificially. That is, if I avoid anything that could disrupt the alignment of the jaw. This means no running, no chewing of any kind, no extended time talking, and I need to give up caffeine because it interferes with bone growth. I nod as I take in her instructions, overwhelmed by the implications of this injury on my work and life in general. In between these care visits, Chris calls the airline to let them know I missed my flight due to a medical emergency and cancels my hotel reservations and the car that was supposed to pick me up from the airport. He lets my boss know what happened and says we'll be in touch with updates once we know more. My boss arranges for another colleague to cover the presentation I was to give at a national conference and tells me to let her know when I'll be back to work.

Over the next week, I get in touch with my primary care physician, and he orders a full workup to determine if an underlying heart issue is what led me to faint. I am relieved when he tells me that everything looks fine, and my fainting spell was likely due to extreme dehydration and exhaustion. He orders me to slow down and rest. I am relieved no underlying heart condition caused me to faint and think maybe this is the wake-up call that I need not to push myself so hard.

For months, my family and friends have been telling me I need to slow down and not work so hard. Even my boss has told me to cut back my overtime, but I feel as if I have little room to do so. I lead the research department at a mid-size company that provides wellness services to employers, and my entire workday is packed with meetings from 8 a.m. until 5 p.m., leaving no time to respond to emails or the half dozen mini crises that come up during the day. The requests for sales support and client travel seem like something I can't turn down. Then there is the need to publish the research my team is doing and to meet my own department's goals. When I explain the dilemma to my boss, she tells me no one can figure this out for me; I simply need to set boundaries and prioritize my work. I appreciate she gives me so much autonomy in my work, but I was hoping for more specific guidance about what responsibilities I might let go of or for more permission to say "no" to some of the demands on my schedule. My problem is that everything feels like a high priority, and I don't feel empowered to push back on the constant requests for client and sales support. I feel stuck.

My Journey from Burnout to Thriving

The meeting with my boss occurred at the end of the workday and I feel overwhelmed and despondent as I drive home. I've kept a journal ever since my teenage years and whenever life throws me a major curveball or problem to solve, I tend to write my way through it. Since my husband is still wrapping up his meetings when I arrive at home, I figure it's a good opportunity to journal about my dilemma.

On paper, it looks as if I had it all: a nice new house with a short commute to work, a loving husband and good friends, and a good job where I felt respected by my peers. Instead, I was burned out and felt increasingly disconnected from my co-workers and most of my friends. My decade-long ascent from an entry-level research associate position to leading the research department was coupled with many organizational changes including mergers, acquisitions, layoffs, and as many executive leadership changes. I felt a constant need to help a revolving door of new bosses understand the value that I and my department brought to the organization. I worked increasingly longer hours to meet an increasing set of demands. The truth was that my work felt like drudgery much of the time, with rare moments of excitement when I was working (usually in evenings and on weekends) on projects valued by the organization but non-essential to my core job.

I had returned to school for my PhD while working full time and had graduated a few years earlier with my degree. It was satisfying to be doing the kind of work that inspired me to go back to get a doctoral degree, but I was exhausted from the effort of completing the degree online while working full time as a researcher. After I graduated, my friends and family urged me to relax and enjoy myself more. I tried working less and socializing more on the weekends. I tried reading books on happiness. I trained for and completed several half marathons. I signed up for a yoga certification course and dropped out when the intensive weekend workshops and required reading conflicted with my business travel.

About two years into my journey, I realized I'd been looking in the wrong places to find fulfillment and rekindle joy in my life. When I dug deeply into what gave me hope and joy and meaning, it came down to rediscovering my purpose in life, asking myself what my values were and if/how I was living them out in my daily life. When I compared my list against my everyday behavior, I was faced with the hard truth that my lifestyle was not a reflection of what I said mattered most to me. As I reflect on this now, it seems so obvious to me that the questions that were surfacing then are common for a mid-career professional in her forties: What is the point of my hard work? What's most important to me? Now that I've achieved all the major goals that I'd set for myself in education, career, and life, why do the achievements feel so empty? Is there something more than this? And perhaps most disturbing, will I ever feel deep, satisfying joy again? The questions I was asking myself were big life questions that pondered the meaning and purpose of life. I felt increasingly isolated and lonely even though I had a supportive network of spouse, family, and friends. I also struggled to reestablish spiritual well-being practices (e.g., daily journaling and reflection on my priorities and values) I'd learned in college but hadn't survived the transitions of marriage, moving to a new state, and entering the professional workplace. At the time, I could sense I needed a big change, but I wasn't sure what kind of change was needed.

My husband was looking to advance his IT career, and when he had the opportunity to be relocated from the Midwest to a larger market, I pledged my full support. Over the course of the next year, my husband and I sold nearly everything that we had and relocated to California for his job with a large software company. My own job change occurred about six months later when I was laid off in a massive reduction-in-force that occurred on the heels of yet another corporate merger.

Due to my advancement to a vice president role two years prior to the layoff, I was privy to information that many others in the organization were not. I had seen the layoff coming and knew my name was on the list for positions to be eliminated, but I didn't believe they'd let me go. I'd always been able to defend the value of the research function in the past and had sustained numerous rounds of layoffs without having to cut a member of my team.

I got the official news of my layoff at the same time as everyone else in the organization. As I shared the news of my departure with my team under the watchful eyes of my latest direct supervisor, I felt a combination of guilt, shame, and relief. As difficult as it was to experience so much change, I embraced it as a chance to begin anew. To live a life that aligned with what I felt mattered most and was an expression of my most deeply held values. To show up in my relationships in a more authentic way. To pursue connection with something bigger than myself. Eventually, I found my way back to the career I loved, and I created my own operating principles to achieve work-life balance.

Unfortunately, my experience of fatigue, burnout, and disengagement from my work has become increasingly common. The questions I was asking myself more than ten years ago seem to come up a lot as employers grapple with higher-than-ever voluntary quit rates and workplace burnout. You may be experiencing this as well and are reading this book from the perspective of someone in desperate need of a workplace that supports your well-being or as a leader seeking new solutions to support the well-being of others. As someone who has walked that dark valley of exhaustion, burnout, and a yearning for more joy, I hope you'll find some comfort in knowing you are not alone as well as inspiration that there is a path toward a more meaningful, connected, and joyful life.

As I write this today, I feel as if I finally cracked the code on how to balance physical, mental, emotional, spiritual, career, and financial well-being. I needed more than a decade to figure this out, and it felt like a journey I had to navigate on my own. I decided to write this book because I am convinced the workplace has a role to play in supporting employees more fully in their well-being journey, including being able to navigate the tough life questions about meaning, purpose, and what matters most in life. I open each chapter of the book with vignettes from my personal well-being journey, which increasingly recognizes the contribution that spiritual well-being played in my ability to find meaning, purpose, connection, and engagement with my work. As I'll discuss further in this book, when I talk about spiritual well-being, I'm talking about having the following: a strong sense of meaning and purpose in life; a sense of connection and belonging; and a connection to something greater than oneself, which is called transcendence. Many workplaces have been reticent to address spirituality as part of a comprehensive approach to worker well-being, and this book proposes an approach that addresses some of the barriers. But why must workplaces broach this uncomfortable territory?

As I'll discuss in Chapter 1, many workplaces are failing to foster an environment that helps their employees to thrive, and it is having a significant impact on the bottom line. A national survey of working Americans found that, in December of 2021, nearly 60% were experiencing burnout, an increase of 20% from the previous year.[1] Though the contributors to diminished mental health may be due to circumstances outside of the workplace, the role of the workplace to buffer and support employees and their families has never been more clearly magnified. My journey from burnout to thriving was largely an exercise in trial and error, but it didn't have to be. While I was experiencing my wake-up call moment more than ten years ago, a robust movement of scientists, researchers, academicians, and practitioners were exploring the role of workplaces to help employees connect with a greater sense of meaning, fulfillment, engagement, and connection in their work. It turns out, an organization can do many things to address the challenges that workers are experiencing with burnout, disengagement, and lack of professional fulfillment.

This book aims to bridge what I've discovered in my more than twenty-five years of research about best practice approaches to workplace health and well-being with the equally large body of research in the management sciences realm of workplace spirituality. Yes, research! Everything proposed in this book is grounded in a solid scientific evidence base and has been field tested in organizations all over the world. But many employers with robust health and well-being initiatives have failed to incorporate some of the practices demonstrated by workplace spirituality researchers to help employees feel more engaged and fulfilled in their work.

I first learned about some of this research as I was editing a special issue of a peer-reviewed journal on the topic of spiritual well-being.[2] There is an increasing openness to spiritual well-being practices within the workplace and I believe the pandemic has increased that openness. Employers are looking for new ways to engage employees and to help them to be their best selves. They want to attract and retain top talent. They want workers to feel engaged and to promote thriving, and they want the increased productivity and performance that comes from that. Though workplace well-being initiatives have been around for decades, many efforts fail to fully address the deeper spiritual elements of what it means to find meaning and purpose in one's work, to cultivate a community of connection and caring with co-workers, and to pursue a connection to that which elicits deep abiding joy and fulfillment. This book aims to help employers address such elements as part of a comprehensive, holistic approach to workplace well-being.

Who Should Read This Book?

If you are responsible for some aspect of employee health and well-being in your organization (e.g., as an executive or manager in a people management or HR role), this book is for you. Just as I experienced my own personal wake-up call ten years ago and started to incorporate spiritual well-being practices into my journey, many employers today are experiencing a wake-up call that their well-being efforts are falling short of addressing employee needs.

After a discussion in Chapter 1, "Wake-Up Call for Employers," about why traditional workplace well-being initiatives are failing to fully address employee needs, I'll outline a more holistic approach to workplace well-being that includes supporting the spiritual well-being of employees. The approach I'll share is grounded in research, and this book will demonstrate how workplace spirituality practices can contribute to business outcomes, such as attraction and retention of top talent, company reputation, global competitiveness, and corporate sustainability. I'll make a case for why next generation workplace well-being needs to address the lack of professional fulfillment that workers are feeling, to address escalating levels of isolation and loneliness, and to create a workplace climate where employees feel valued and appreciated at work, have hope for their future, and have access to experiences that tap into their creativity and fuel joy in their lives.

As I'll explain in Chapter 2, "Workplace Well-Being Requires Collaboration," this necessitates a multi-disciplinary approach that brings together professionals in diverse functions or roles, such as human resources, organizational learning, leadership development, occupational health and safety, risk management, facilities management, and diversity, equity, and inclusion (DEI). This chapter provides a brief overview of the workplace spirituality research grounded in management science and discusses some potential underlying reasons for and implications resulting from a lack of integration between the workplace spirituality and workplace health and well-being fields.

Research indicates many workplaces have been reluctant to use the term "spirituality" as part of their approach to worker well-being and Chapter 3, "A Framework for Comprehensive, Holistic Well-Being," will tackle the issue of terminology as well as introduce a framework for a more comprehensive and holistic approach to workplace well-being that includes spirituality. It also details how to address holistic well-being at four levels: individual, interpersonal/group, organizational, and societal while also addressing the special role that leaders play in creating cultures of well-being. These opening chapters aim to create context and set the stage for the subsequent chapters.

Part Two of the book discusses each of the three elements of workplace spirituality that will be introduced in Chapter 3, including fostering "a culture of individual purpose" (Chapter 4), "a culture of connection and belonging" (Chapter 5), and "a culture of transcendence" (Chapter 6). Each of these three chapters are organized similarly, starting with an introduction of what it means to address the element of focus, providing research supporting its link to individual well-being as well as its link to business outcomes, addressing how to apply the research to practice, and featuring how organizations are implementing elements of workplace spirituality in real-world business settings. A final chapter in Part Two, "Workplace Well-Being Across Four Levels of Influence" (Chapter 7), will further detail how to incorporate evidence-based approaches across each of the four levels of influence introduced in Chapter 3.

Part Three of this book focuses on implementation of the framework and the levels of intervention addressed in Part Two, beginning with Chapter 8, "Redesigning Your Workplace Well-Being Blueprint." Chapter 8 offers a brief, more general primer on how to design evidence-based workplace well-being initiatives (including those that incorporate spiritual well-being) and which are integrated into the fabric of the organization. As Chapter 7 will address, the success of any endeavor aimed at influencing organizational culture requires substantial leadership buy-in and support. This includes development of a strategic plan, measurable objectives, measurement and evaluation, and ongoing process improvement. No matter the scope of your well-being initiatives, this chapter will speak to the foundational steps that support the development of an effective approach.

Gaining and sustaining leadership support is bolstered when the proposed approach has been demonstrated to be effective. Chapter 9, "Whole Person Well-Being Is Better for Business," aims to summarize the research and connect the dots among workplace spirituality, workplace well-being, and outcomes at the individual and organizational levels. Special attention will be paid to the challenging issues identified in Chapter 1 including worker burnout, engagement, retention, turnover, and performance.

The book closes with the final chapter in this section, "Aligning Vision, Solution, and Results" (Chapter 10), which discusses using a storytelling approach to achieve and sustain alignment between these elements within the dynamic nature of the modern workplace, which often results in rapidly shifting priorities that challenge any initiative to deliver on envisioned expectations.

Bridging Research and Practice

As a researcher who was once a workplace wellness program practitioner, you can rest assured that I'll focus on applied practices that work in the real world. There is substantial research to support the adoption of spiritual well-being practices, but most employers and wellness practitioners know nothing about this research. They don't know a solid business case exists to support paying attention to spiritual well-being. And they don't know that it's possible to address it in a way that honors DEI as well as complies with HR policies. After delving into the robust research in this area, I believe adding spiritual well-being to workplace practices is the most meaningful way to help employees feel engaged, connected, valued, and professionally/personally fulfilled. More than two years after the pandemic dramatically shifted the nature of what it means to report to work, we continue to be in a state of flux. The ambiguity of the future of the workplace is an opportunity to try new things. We must boldly experiment with assurance that missteps will occur and must rely on a growth mindset to support the exploration of the uncharted territory that lies before us. This is the time to try something new because the old way of doing things is insufficient to address the emerging needs of our time. Turn the page, let your curiosity inspire you to reimagine how things could be, and take a courageous step forward into oceans deep, trusting that solid ground will rise up to meet you.

PART ONE

A Reimagined Approach

CHAPTER 1

Wake-Up Call for Employers

"There needs to be a shift in consciousness;
there needs to be an absolute wake-up call
before society can actually make the kind of
incredibly significant changes that need to happen."

— ANNIE LENNOX

A Familiar Scenario

I am walking on my treadmill in time to take a call with my friend, David, who is also eschewing the common video call in favor of a walking meeting. Several years ago, I started the habit of taking one-on-one calls that did not require me to be at my computer as a walking phone call and have slowly influenced my family members and professional peers to do the same. It's one of many ways that I've integrated well-being into my largely sedentary work as a researcher.

David and I are enrolled in an online course about navigating mid-life transitions, and he confided to me several months ago that he was considering a job change from a somewhat operational director role to a more strategic role in the health and well-being space. After an initial catch-up on lighter topics, I shift the conversation into deeper territory by asking how things are going with his work.

"Funny you should ask," David replies. "I just happen to have a meeting with my executive leaders at the end of the day today, and I think I'm going to give my resignation."

"What?!" I can't keep the surprise out of my voice and nearly trip while walking on the treadmill. I slow the pace a bit and regain my composure before saying in a more neutral tone, "I know you've been considering a job change, but what's precipitated this meeting?"

David tells me about a series of communications he's had in recent weeks and how he's feeling the senior executive team has not been taking his recommendations about needing to address staff well-being more seriously. "You know, I took this job because I thought the leaders in this organization were serious about investing in the health and well-being of their workers, but every time I make a recommendation, they make some excuse about it not being the right time. On the heels of the latest corporate directive to launch another initiative focused on bolstering market share, I am at the point where I can no longer continue in my role. I requested this meeting to initiate discussions about my transition out of the organization."

As we continue our conversation, I reflect on a pattern I've seen emerging among my peer group over the past year. David is one of half a dozen professional peers I know who was serving in a senior leadership position at the start of the year and then initiated a departure from their organization because its direction was not aligned with their personal values or met their needs for professional fulfillment. In addition to those, I know several peers who are burned out and are looking to take a break to recover their energy and strength. David's story reminded me about the growing dissatisfaction I had experienced in my career when I felt my work wasn't making a meaningful difference in the world. I suspect it's a scenario you can relate to as someone experiencing similar circumstances or dealing with the organizational challenge of attracting and retaining top talent. As I'll address in future chapters, these challenges are not insurmountable.

A Wake-Up Call for Employers

According to the US Bureau of Labor Statistics, voluntary turnover rates are a growing trend and one that is causing alarm in numerous sectors. Dubbed "the Great Resignation" by Anthony Klotz, an associate professor of management at Texas A&M University, millions of people took steps in 2021 to leave their current employers, including frontline workers and senior business leaders. In November 2021 alone, 4.5 million US workers voluntarily quit their jobs, contributing to the highest quit rate ever reported.[3] Recent research in 2022 suggests this trend will continue, with more employees considering quitting their jobs this year than in 2021, especially for younger workers.[4] According to Gartner, a global research and advisory firm, employees are demanding more in return for the time, effort, and intellectual capital they bring to their employer. They want to be valued for their contributions and ". . . to be seen as complex human beings with rich, full lives."[5] Employers who have prided themselves for offering a competitive salary, a safe place to work, and a large array of benefits are finding it's no longer enough to attract and retain top talent. Workers in a variety of positions from hourly nail technicians to specialty practice physicians are leaving their jobs in search of a more enriching life.[6]

Of those who remain at work, a significant number say they are experiencing burnout. In a 2021 Visier national survey of

1,000 full-time workers, 89% reported experiencing burnout over the past year.[7] Burnout is characterized by emotional exhaustion, decreased personal accomplishment, and feelings of indifference, cynicism, and negative attitudes toward others.[8] Though burnout is often misunderstood as a problem primarily plaguing people in blue-collar jobs that entail rote work, and little autonomy in their work, it can also occur in professional workers who initially enjoyed their work and were passionate about their career and successful in achieving their goals.[9]

Employers are concerned about burnout because higher levels of unaddressed burnout are related to higher turnover and absenteeism rates as well as increased use of high-cost health care services. It's also linked to poor employee performance.[10] A majority of employees (70%) who are experiencing some level of burnout say they would leave their job for one with a company that offered resources, policies, and benefits intended to reduce burnout. When researchers asked about the factors contributing to burnout, it's no surprise that workload and lack of control in one's job contributed. These are the usual suspects when it comes to work-related stress and burnout. However, a third of employees attributed burnout to having a toxic workplace culture. This includes an environment characterized by office gossip, sexism, bullying, and incivility at work.

Though burnout represents a negative psychological state, it is highly related to the more positive concept of worker engagement, which is characterized by high levels of energy, dedication, and involvement and immersion in one's work.[11] If you've ever found yourself caught up in a work project or task when you felt totally immersed in your work, lost track of time and ended the workday feeling a sense of accomplishment and satisfaction, you've experienced high levels of work engagement. But highly engaged employees are also at risk for burnout because if they don't balance their focus on work performance with an equal focus on recovery and self-care, they can experience burnout too.

Gallup reports indicate that only 36% of US employees are engaged in their work and workplace,[12] which means that the other 64% of workers are experiencing some level of disengagement. Employers concerned about turnover rates and worker performance care about worker engagement because lower levels are linked to absenteeism, turnover, safety incidents, worker theft, and quality defects; higher levels of engagement are linked to improved productivity, customer loyalty levels, and company profitability.[13] Most critically for employers concerned about attraction and retention of top talent due to the Great Resignation, highly engaged employees are 87% less likely to leave their job. This has substantial implications for organizational profitability. One organization estimates that US employers spend nearly $3 million per day searching for new employees or replacement workers.[14] Another estimates that employers in the US lose more than $5,000 every time an employee leaves the company.[15] What's also concerning are employee disengagement rates because 74% of actively disengaged employees are seeking another job. Recent 2021 Gallup reports indicate 15% of US employees are actively disengaged, resulting in productivity losses equal to 18% of the worker's annual salary.[16]

Turnover rates and worker productivity are not the only issues keeping business leaders up at night. US adult suicide rates and mental health issues are also rising. A 2020 report by the US Centers for Disease Control and Prevention (CDC) reported that nearly 53% of US adults reported having an adverse mental or behavioral health condition, and 11% reported having seriously considered suicide in the past month.[17] National suicide rates reached a fifty-year high in September of 2021, with 44,000 Americans dying by suicide each year.[18] The latest report by Mental Health America (2021) reported that nearly 5% of US adults (that's one in twenty!) reported having serious thoughts of suicide, and this number has increased every year since 2011. A 2014 study on work-related suicides states there is a direct connection between workplace distress and employee suicide.[19] These deaths from despair reveal a deep sense of hopelessness and suffering, which have only been compounded since 2020.

As I am writing this book, the world is still reeling from more than two years of the COVID-19 pandemic, ongoing racial injustice and political divisiveness following the murder of George Floyd, global climate change, and diminished mental health as we deal with the cumulative impact of ongoing change, loss, and ambiguity about the future. In public health parlance, this is referred to as a syndemic because these occurrences are happening concurrently, and they synergize and make the others worse. The syndemic has impacted nearly every aspect of daily life, from what's available in the grocery store to how we engage in our communities to how far out we dare to make plans for vacations, birthdays, weddings, or even dinner with friends on the weekend.

Some of the most profound changes have occurred with the nature of our working lives. Some lost their jobs, and others were asked to work mandatory overtime shifts. Some continued to report to the workplace with fear and trepidation for their safety, and others were required to work from kitchen tables, spare bedrooms, or the garage. Many working parents struggled to manage their own work demands while also helping children navigate online learning and attending to the needs of their aging parents. As if these disruptions weren't challenging enough for employers, increased awareness of racial injustice and the accumulation of so much loss and change required employers to create space for employees to have authentic conversations about the challenges they were experiencing.

The state of the workplace is in uncharted territory; so many unknowns and ambiguity is scary and disorienting. Attending to the health and well-being of the workforce has taken center stage, but even workers and organizations with the highest levels of resources and resiliency are cracking beneath the strain and burden of the challenges that must be addressed. Individuals, teams, and organizations are struggling with a combination of individual, organizational, and societal factors that are largely out of their control. So, what can be done within the realm of workplace well-being to meet the emerging needs of our time? It requires an expanded approach and a shift in how and why organizations invest in workplace well-being initiatives.

Traditional Approaches to Workplace Well-Being

Up until recently, many business leaders may have viewed workplace well-being programs as a non-essential perk or as a strategy to contain health care costs. A 2015 study of US business leaders found that approximately one-third of them viewed employee health as a cost that needed to be contained rather than as a core business strategy.[20] More recent data suggest a sea change in thinking has occurred. Qualitative interviews with twenty CEOs of large companies found most of them agreed that organizational health is dependent on the well-being of its people, and this was before the global pandemic.[21]

A 2021 survey of more than 200 HR executives identified employee well-being and mental health as their number one strategic priority.[22]

Though a majority of employers say they are doing something to invest in employee well-being, only 17% were investing in a comprehensive approach to workforce well-being in 2017.[23] Many workplace well-being programs offered in the United States have largely focused on individualistic approaches, which place the onus of responsibility for well-being on the employee. I'm a case in point. As I mentioned in the Introduction, when I was experiencing burn-out, disengagement, and a lack of fulfillment in a previous role, my supervisor told me that it was my problem to solve. I alone needed to figure out how to balance my priorities and set boundaries. I alone had to figure out how to reinvigorate my work with a greater sense of meaning and strengthen my sense of connection to co-workers. Dr. Jennifer Moss argues that organizational culture contributes significantly to burnout, necessitating a more systemic approach.[24] And this book aims to help employers understand how to take a more systemic approach in addressing holistic worker well-being. This begins when employers recognize the significant role that workplace culture has on worker well-being.

A more comprehensive, holistic approach to worker well-being addresses organizational factors, such as leadership expectations and behaviors, workplace policies and processes, and the workplace environment. This includes addressing workplace spirituality, which I'll discuss in Chapter 3. Subsequent chapters will detail the measurable, objective workplace spirituality practices that organizations can implement in the areas of leadership behaviors, workplace policies and processes, and the workplace environment. Studies have shown that workers with a low sense of spirituality were more likely to experience burnout.[25] For employers seeking to get more value out of their investment in workplace well-being and address emerging issues, such as burnout and lack of professional fulfillment, research shows many organizations will require a more comprehensive approach than they have been implementing.[26]

Many employer programs have also been limited in the scope of well-being that is addressed, primarily with an emphasis on physical wellness, which translates into fitness classes, reduced-cost gym memberships, balancing unhealthy vending and onsite catering options with more nutritious foods, and providing onsite biometric health screenings. Policies and programs have been targeted to help smokers quit using tobacco and help those with chronic conditions manage their health. Some of the more innovative efforts have also incorporated better sleep practices into their programs.

In terms of mental and emotional health, traditional approaches to well-being have focused on stress management or resiliency programs that workers must take advantage of largely amid their busy lives outside of work. Some employers might provide onsite meditation classes or quiet relaxation areas that allow employees to decompress during the workday, assuming that employees who most need a break from a demanding job will take advantage of them. There is also a growing number of employers offering programs and resources to address financial well-being, which makes sense because financial concerns are a major source of stress for many employees. Financial well-being offerings might include debt reduction services, budgeting classes, or access to a financial planning professional.

The expansion of attention beyond physical wellness has led many organizations to rename their wellness programs to "well-being initiatives."[27] But even with these expanded offerings, most employers report it's not enough to stem the tide of employee burnout, increasing turnover, and disengagement. A 2021 survey of more than 500 US employers found that 98% were planning to offer or expand at least one employee benefit, specifically around child/ senior care benefits, flexible scheduling policies, and mental health services.[28] This is welcome news for professionals that have been trying for years to get executive leadership support for employee well-being programs. Professionals, like my friend David, had to begin a resignation process before his leaders took him seriously.

Next Generation Approaches to Workplace Well-Being

It's terrific that employers are starting to broaden the spectrum of issues addressed as part of their well-being initiatives, but today's challenges require more than an expanded menu of programs, resources, and workplace perks. Employers need to do more than raise awareness and ask employees to enroll in educational programs to enhance their well-being. Now, more than ever, employees are trying to make sense out of the world around them. They are asking big questions, like "What really matters to me?" and "How do I prioritize the things that bring me joy and fulfillment?"

Next generation workplace well-being needs to address the lack of professional fulfillment workers are feeling. Employers need to address escalating levels of isolation and loneliness by identifying new ways to help employees feel connected to one another as part of their work. Workers also need to feel included, valued, and appreciated at work; to have hope for their future; and to have access to experiences that tap into their creativity and fuel joy in their lives. As I'll explain in the coming chapters, the workplace spirituality field has sought to address these issues, and I'll make a case for why it is in business leaders' best interests to address these needs within the workplace.

My primary purpose for this book is to inspire business leaders and workplace health and well-being practitioners to include aspects of workplace spirituality in their organization's approach to employee well-being. My secondary purpose is to identify from the research what it means to address workplace spirituality in a way that invites people of all faiths and wisdom traditions (including employees who do not identify as religious) to pursue a more holistic well-being journey. As has always been the case with workplace well-being, employers cannot choose what the well-being journey looks like for any individual, but they can create the conditions that inspire employees to get on a path toward well-being. To that end, my language aims to be broad and inclusive, which aligns with many thought leaders in the workplace spirituality field.

It's time to consider a more holistic approach instead of the traditional package of programs and perks. Facing the challenges of this moment in time may seem like a daunting task for any workplace well-being initiative to attain. To be sure, designing effective initiatives is hard work, requiring exceptional levels of organizational commitment from leaders at all levels. Thankfully, decades of research exists to guide us forward. In my more than twenty-five years of work in the workplace well-being field, I've seen employers of all sizes design and implement initiatives that have made a difference in the lives of their employees and returned value to the organization. Keep reading to learn how your organization can incorporate evidence-based strategies into a broader definition of well-being that includes the spiritual well-being of workers.

CHAPTER 1

HIGHLIGHTS

- Voluntary quit rates and levels of employee burnout reached unprecedented levels in 2021.

- Heightened concerns over employee mental, emotional, and physical well-being has made organizational investment in employee well-being a top strategic business priority.

- Employees are looking for more meaning, purpose, and fulfillment in their work. They want to feel more connected, valued, respected, and included by their peers. Most traditional workplace well-being initiatives fail to help employees address these issues.

- Though many employers report investing in employee well-being, most organizations are not taking a comprehensive approach.

- A next generation approach to workplace well-being addresses organizational environment and culture as well as offers individual programs to help employees thrive in their work. It also addresses holistic well-being across mental, emotional, physical, and spiritual dimensions.

- Robust scientific evidence supports a more comprehensive and holistic approach to next generation employee well-being initiatives. This book aims to help employers incorporate evidence-based workplace spirituality practices into comprehensive health and well-being efforts.

Workplace Well-Being Requires Collaboration

"Think multidisciplinary!
Problems, by definition, cross many academic disciplines."

— LUCAS REMMERSWAAL

Hidden in Plain Sight

Ten years ago, as I was recovering from the trauma of the broken jaw suffered after collapsing from work-related exhaustion and fatigue, I began to do some deep thinking and journaling about how I might change the trajectory of my work and life plan. I'd recently finished my doctoral program and was happy to be conducting research studies and successfully getting them published in my industry's leading professional journals. This is what I'd worked so hard to achieve, but the victory felt hollow. Most of the business leaders I talked to were not interested in reading research articles, and some of the studies I was most proud of began to be publicly attacked by critics of workplace wellness programs. Piled on top of that discouragement was the growing fixation of the industry on contractual performance guarantees, which my department was made responsible for negotiating, calculating, and defending.

As I grew increasingly dissatisfied with the work that occupied my days, I spent my nights reading books on happiness and imagined a different future. This led me back to reconnecting with my faith, and I realized that I could find renewed purpose in my work and life by seeking to align my everyday activities with my values and beliefs. I wasn't a member of a church because we moved to a new community during my doctoral program, and I hadn't been able to make time to start visiting local churches. I'd been part of a vibrant faith group during my undergraduate years in Wisconsin and none of the many churches I visited after moving to Minnesota seemed like the right fit. I reread some of my favorite books from a faith-based leadership training camp I'd attended in college and introduced prayer into my daily commute. I enrolled in a yoga teacher certification course, which exposed me to the philosophical side of the practice. I also started a daily gratitude journal. After many months, I felt as if I was slowly recovering my previous energy and enthusiasm for my work. Then I contemplated doing more research on approaches to wellness that incorporated elements of spirituality. After experiencing for myself how important it was to better align my beliefs and values with my daily actions in work and in life, I wondered if adding this aspect into wellness programs might be helpful for the employees our programs were designed to serve.

I approached a few senior leaders in my organization and was told that faith-based approaches were not something that employers would embrace and they discouraged me from further exploration on the topic as part of my work. But my interest in it continued, and I began to incorporate faith-based wellness strategies into my personal wellness journey. It was not until I revisited the topic of faith-based approaches nearly ten years later that I discovered a whole area of scholarship and research existed on workplace spirituality. In fact, when I'd first inquired about the idea of a faith-based approach to workplace wellness, the research on workplace spirituality was at its peak. How could I have missed it? Hundreds of research studies, numerous scholars, and even a professional association with journals devoted to the topic. As I would come to discover, I was looking in the wrong places and using the wrong search terms. I also learned that a faith-based approach to well-being was a subset beneath the larger umbrella of workplace spirituality. Many scholars in the field advocate for a more general approach to spiritual well-being that includes those who identify as spiritual but not religious, as I'll discuss further in the next chapter.

A Tale of Two Siloed Sectors

Spiritual well-being has long been on the radar in the world of wellness, as indicated by its inclusion in the National Wellness Institute's 1976 model, which incorporates the spiritual dimension.[29] The model depicts the various domains of individual well-being, which organizational and community influences can support. Ten years later, the inaugural issue of the *American Journal of Health Promotion* (which would become one of the leading scholarly journals for the field of workplace health promotion) featured a commentary by Larry Chapman, calling for health promotion (aka, wellness) practitioners to include spirituality in their organizations' wellness initiatives.[30] More than thirty years after that article, I interviewed Larry about the progress that had been made in the field.[31] Even though he acknowledged the increasing acknowledgement of the spiritual dimension in employer-sponsored wellness programs, he felt efforts had not been explicitly approached as a unified domain called "spiritual health." When pressed about some of the reasons for this observation, he suggested several. Of the five possible explanations he offered for the lack of a cohesive or integrated approach to spiritual health in workplace wellness initiatives, the one that seems to resonate most among other experts that I've talked to is that the term spirituality seems to invite controversy or conflict because most people confuse its distinction with religion, which workplaces tend to avoid talking about.

> The concept of "spirit" has its roots for most Americans, in a biblical worldview, and our post-modern and post-Christian society seems to be conflicted about comparing notes on spiritual perceptions. There is also some confusion about the difference between spirituality and religion. In other words, the use of the term "spiritual" in spiritual health raises the unwelcome possibility of potential controversy or conflict.[32]

Since that interview was published, I've continued to explore this area as I've felt drawn to find more meaning and purpose in my personal and professional life. I believe my personal exploration mirrors a broader hunger observed across many workplaces today. In some sectors, we have seen more significant integration of faith, religion, and spirituality into health and well-being programs. For example, many universities and some health care systems include spirituality as one dimension of their well-being initiatives. My early searches of public health scholarly literature found many examples of faith-based wellness programs, which were often offered within the context of a community or church setting with a focus on a specific religion. This was discouraging for me because publicly traded and government-oriented workplaces are unlikely to offer programs associated with a specific faith tradition. I realized after many months and numerous forays into the research databases that I'd been using the wrong search terms to find my way to the scholars who were very explicitly addressing the role of faith, religion, and spirituality in the world of work. It was the search term "workplace spirituality" that finally landed me into an ocean of research articles and introduced me to numerous thought leaders who have been passionately studying, teaching, and leading for decades.

I learned that the first management journal articles on workplace spirituality were published in 1994.[33] Mainstream media articles emerged a short time later, such as the 1995 *Business Week* article that asked, ". . . can spirituality enlighten the bottom line?"[34] That same year, industry and media articles featured workplace spirituality practices at Boeing, Tom's of Maine, Ford Motor Company, and many others. Academic scholarship took off and several years later the Academy of Management (AOM) founded the Management, Spirituality & Religion (MSR) interest group. By 2004, one empirical research review identified 187 studies combining the topics of spirituality and management.[35] The study of this area gained more credibility with the establishment of the *Journal of Management, Spirituality, and Religion*[36], and by 2015, a total of 988 studies was yielded in a similar search.[37]

As I began to wade through books and research studies, I regretted my lack of persistence when I first became curious about the integration of spirituality and the workplace more than ten years earlier. Again, I asked myself how I could have missed this body of work. It's a question I posed first to the thought leaders I knew in the workplace well-being field, and it was somewhat reassuring when one person after another told me they hadn't been aware of this workplace spirituality movement either. In fact, they encouraged me to think more about how to integrate what I was discovering into my knowledge of workplace well-being best practices.

One of the challenges I had to overcome as I started exploring workplace spirituality was my discomfort with unfamiliar language, concepts, and research. I was afraid of appearing uninformed and lacking credibility when I approached researchers and thought leaders to discuss how our work aligned. It takes a healthy dose of humility for people in a respected leadership role to disclose what they don't know. I had to learn to get comfortable asking questions and admitting my lack of familiarity with commonly used theories, approaches, and well-known researchers in another field.

Once I gained the courage to start reaching out to the workplace spirituality thought leaders, they confirmed my observation that these two fields have remained siloed. One of the reasons may be that the workplace spirituality movement has been focused on management theory and leadership development. The movement helped spawn or inform other movements devoted to servant leadership, ethics in management, and Conscious Capitalism. When I introduced my area of scholarship (workplace well-being) to scholars in the workplace spirituality movement, they were confused. What did employee wellness have to do with Conscious Capitalism, conscious leadership, or corporate sustainability?

A Call for Collaboration

As I reflect on my initial inquiries into the integration of spirituality and workplace well-being, I am reminded that my organization and most of my peers were not yet working in a multi-disciplinary way. For example, we didn't regularly engage organizational leadership, development, and effectiveness professionals. That's changed in the past decade. Most guidance on best practice approaches to workplace well-being encourages collaboration with leaders across the corporate functions of occupational health and safety, human resources, compensation and benefits, facilities management, and organizational learning and development.[38] Laura Putnam refers to this as a "da Vinci approach" based on Leonardo da Vinci's approach to combining multiple disciplines in his work as an artist, inventor, engineer, and architect. Putnam's book, *Workplace Wellness that Works,* offers workplace well-being practitioners numerous examples and suggestions on how to build cross-departmental, interdisciplinary solutions to better support employee well-being.[39]

Brandon Peele, cofounder of Unity Lab, exhorts us to ". . . come together across differences to serve an aligned vision, empowering cross-functional teams to achieve common goals and objectives and actively nurture care, trust, and autonomy . . . . No single business unit or function can address workload, belonging, inclusion, productivity, flourishing, innovation, wellness, employee engagement, or attraction/retention. They all must align in order to create true systemic and culture change."[40]

But what does it mean to collaborate across disciplines? Michael Schrage defines collaboration as "the process of shared creation." It results from ". . . two or more individuals with complementary skills interacting to create a shared understanding that none had previously possessed or could have come to on their own."[41] Taking this definition to heart, we can move forward knowing that we don't need to have all the answers but rather an attitude of mutual respect for and belief in one another's abilities to work from different perspectives toward a shared goal. Having surrounded myself with people far smarter and more talented than me for the duration of my career, I've learned to lean into the discomfort of unfamiliar territory. Collaboration requires courage but also humility, curiosity, and infectious enthusiasm for shared discovery. What I've come to discover is even the most accomplished thought leaders and researchers relish the opportunity to collaborate with like-minded individuals. The key is to align ourselves around common challenges and objectives.

Bridging Workplace Spirituality and Workplace Well-Being

As I familiarized myself with the workplace well-being and workplace spirituality research and talked with other scholars, I identified some similar challenges. One challenge is related to language and definitions. In both fields, those interested in spirituality have said no common understanding or definition of spirituality exists. A chief limitation related to this lack of a definition is confusion about how spirituality differs from religion, a topic many organizations avoid for fear of appearing to endorse a specific religious tradition. Another limitation is around measurement of spirituality. Lack of a common understanding of the concept has led to the proliferation of measurement tools, which is a challenge when it comes to synthesizing the research. This lack of consensus around definition and measurement requires people seeking to address spirituality to begin by sharing their definition of the term. Some research reviews limit their synthesis to studies using the same measurement tool to assess spirituality, which is helpful for generalizing a body of research measuring the same thing but less helpful to compare and contrast study findings. Future chapters provide guidance on how to address issues related to language, definitions, and measurement of spirituality.

Another shared challenge of both fields is the predominant focus on individuals as the unit of analysis in research studies, which limits our understanding about how addressing spirituality within the workplace influences interpersonal and group dynamics as well as organizational outcomes. What works for one person may not work for groups of people, and the accumulation of individual benefits may not translate to group or organizational outcomes. Overcoming this challenge is difficult because testing interventions using the group or the organization as the unit for analysis in research requires the identification of meaningful comparison groups or organizations. Thankfully, emerging research in the workplace well-being and workplace spirituality fields has examined group and organizational outcomes. Chapter 9 provides a summary of research studies linking workplace spirituality to individual, group, and organizational outcomes.

A final common challenge recognized by experts in both fields is the need to translate research more effectively into practice. Researchers are required to publish their studies in peer-reviewed scholarly journals, where they speak in academic terms and put more emphasis on articulating how the research design was potentially flawed and how this limits the interpretation of results than on a discussion about how the results can inform practical application in the real world. This book aims to bring together in one place specific, actionable practices that employers can implement to create an effective, comprehensive approach to workplace well-being. One that includes addressing spiritual well-being.

While overcoming such problems will take many dedicated scholars and practitioners years to address, this book aims to build a bridge to bring these two fields together. The chapters that follow provide initial guidance on how to integrate workplace spirituality into a comprehensive approach to workplace health and well-being and to serve as a starting point for fruitful new collaborations across multiple disciplines.

CHAPTER 2

HIGHLIGHTS

- Spirituality has long been recognized as an essential facet of a holistic approach to employee well-being, but most workplaces have not addressed this dimension.

- Many business leaders are uncomfortable talking about spirituality due to a lack of understanding about how it is distinct from religion. Any discussion about addressing spirituality must begin by addressing how it differs from religion.

- Decades of research support the importance of addressing spirituality as part of an effective approach to whole-person well-being.

- The fields of workplace well-being and workplace spirituality have been largely siloed, requiring a more collaborative approach.

- This book provides guidance to workplace well-being professionals interested in expanding their efforts to include workplace spirituality.

A Framework for Comprehensive, Holistic Well-Being

"We are not human beings having a spiritual experience.
We are spiritual beings having a human experience."

— PIERRE TEILHARD DE CHARDIN

Coming to Terms with Terms

I'm about to initiate a scheduled call with a professional research peer, Mike, who is interested in catching up with me to learn how my self-imposed twelve-month sabbatical is going. I'd decided years ago to pursue a non-working sabbatical concurrent with my fiftieth birthday, which would happen in a few months. While I was continuing to participate in occasional advisory board calls, I had quit my job as vice president of research for a non-profit so I would have the freedom to pursue whatever interested me.

As I prepare for the call, I wonder for the nth time how much I should tell him about my new area of interest. I breathe a brief prayer for discernment and dial his number. After the typical updates about recent travel and what we're observing in our communities as the COVID-19 pandemic continues, the conversation turns to my sabbatical work.

"I've been doing a lot of reading," I begin. "It's been a joy to follow my curiosity from one book to the next and I'm going through a book a week, on average. On the rare weeks where I don't have calls or advisory board commitments, I can get through a book every day or two."

Mike laughs. "That sounds like you. You've always been a bookworm. Is there a specific theme to your reading? What are you most curious about?"

I pause and decide to answer the question authentically. "You might recall that in 2019, I edited a special section for the American Journal of Health Promotion *on the topic of spiritual well-being as part of workplace well-being programs. I wanted to revisit that topic area and started some new searches to see what's emerged in the research during the past year."*

Mike is silent for a moment, then encourages me to continue. "And what did you find?"

I take a deep breath and continue. "I was surprised to stumble upon a huge body of work related to workplace spirituality. Much of it seems to have come out of the management sciences sector with initiatives related to servant leadership, Conscious Capitalism, and conscious leadership. I'm not seeing much integration of this work into workplace well-being, and I've been trying to discover why. In between books, I've been inter-viewing consultants and thought leaders working in this space. I have a lot of discovery left to do, but I can't seem to make a dent in the number of books available on the topic of workplace spirituality. For every book I finish, there are two more referenced or recommended to me."

I pause, eager for Mike's reaction. "Well, the topic of spirituality isn't coming up in my conversations with leaders." I note his cautious tone as he continues. "I'm probably hearing more about purpose and mental health than anything. I think spirituality is a big turn-off for leaders in the business world because their mind immediately leaps to religion and there's the whole separation of church and state issue in the back of their minds. If you decide to focus on this work, I'd recommend using different terms when you talk to business leaders about it."

The Limitations of Language

Mike's reaction during our conversation is no surprise, and many of the peers I talk with about it agree that most business leaders are uncomfortable with the word "spirituality." Consultants and scholars doing work in the workplace spirituality space say that it's important to begin any discussion about spirituality by first distinguishing it from religion.

Dr. Judi Neal's book *Creating Enlightened Organizations: Four Gateways to Spirit at Work* suggests you don't have to use spiritual language to take a spiritual approach to business.[42] When she conducts workshops with business leaders, she often begins with a useful differentiation exercise. She asks each workshop participant to take a sheet of paper and divide it into two columns, with the word "religion" above one column and the word "spirituality" in the other. Start with the "religion" column and freely write every term that comes to mind in response to that word. After a minute or so, move to the "spirituality" column and list all the words that come to mind in response. You might consider pausing here and completing this exercise for yourself.

Next, she has small groups of participants at each table discuss the similarities and differences between the two concepts, noting where some terms or concepts seem to overlap. Then she brings the groups back together and invites large group discussion about the patterns they observed and the implications of their observations. She ends the exercise with discussion about the relationship between religion and work and the relationship between spirituality and work. If you paused your reading to complete this activity yourself, what commonalities and differences did you observe in your lists? What are the implications as you consider applying workplace spirituality research to your organization's well-being initiatives?

There is a clear lack of consensus about definitions and distinctions between religion, faith, and spirituality among experts in the field of workplace spirituality. Each definition contributes something new to our understanding, particularly when it is operationalized into a measurement tool that is used in research. Some researchers even disagree about whether it's possible or necessary to define spirituality. How do you describe or measure the ineffable? It's like trying to describe the beauty and majesty of the Himalayan Mountains to an individual who has been blind their whole life. Words fail to convey the awe and inspiration the image evokes.

I don't intend to introduce a new definition of spirituality into a crowded field of exceptional candidates, but it does help to understand the etymology of these terms that have become so heavily burdened, sometimes beyond their original meaning. The word "religion" has its roots in the Latin term "religio," which references the interaction between humans and some aspect of the divine. It follows that religion focuses on how human beings think about, express, or act upon their beliefs about their relationship with the divine.

The word "spirit" is derived from the Latin words "spirare" (to breathe) and "spiritus" (the breath). It follows that "spirit" has something to do with the energy or force that upholds all life. A Google.com search of "spirit definition" yields more than 3.4 billion results! Common definitions offered by Google Dictionary include: ". . . the nonphysical part of a person which is the seat of emotions and character; the soul" or ". . . the nonphysical part of a person regarded as their true self and as capable of surviving physical death or separation." Roger Gill, a psychologist and leadership studies scholar, explains that ". . . spirit is what drives people. It is a synergy of meaning, purpose, beliefs and values, a sense of community and belonging, and a sense of value or worth in one's life that together animate us in what we seek and do and thereby leads to our fulfillment and happiness."[43]

Distinguishing Spirituality from Religion

The word "spirituality" is related to religion but constitutes a broader concept, which may include an individual's beliefs about the nature of the universe, including the existence or lack of a universal transcendent force. It is, therefore, possible for an atheist (someone who believes there is no God or gods) to experience spirituality. The Fetzer Institute posits ". . . spirituality is a complex, diverse, and nuanced phenomenon that people of all spiritual and religious self-identifications experience."[44] Its 2020 study of spirituality in the United States found ". . . there is both a depth and diversity of spirituality within and outside of faith traditions that isn't yet reflected in our main cultural narratives. Paradoxically, recognizing this diversity allows a common thread to emerge, one that reveals it is human to be spiritual and engaging in this spirituality can engender a greater good."

Fetzer's identification of spirituality as a common thread within us lays the foundation for workplaces to recognize the fundamental importance of addressing it. According to Fetzer's 2020 study, more than eight out of ten people consider themselves spiritual to some extent and six in ten aspire to be more spiritual. The researchers encourage us to invite people of all spiritual and religious backgrounds into conversation about what spirituality means to them and to understand how it can contribute positively to our world.

McClintock and colleagues conducted a study with participants representing a diversity of religious affiliations including Christianity, Islam, Hinduism, Buddhism, and the category of nonreligious or spiritual-but-not-religious. They found people shared five common spiritual phenotypes: altruism, love of others as oneself, sense of Oneness, practice of sacred transcendence, and adherence to a moral code. The researchers concluded that ". . . while the formation of spirituality is impacted by diverse cultures and traditions, the seat of spiritual perception is innate."[45]

Dr. Lisa Miller is a clinical psychologist, a researcher, and a professor who has been studying the role of spirituality in mental health. After decades of research, she asserts that ". . . all humans are universally equipped with a capacity for spirituality and our brains become more resilient and robust as a result of it."[46] As I read her research, I became convinced that addressing spirituality is a missing aspect to most of the resiliency initiatives I've come across in the workplace. In her work, she's been advocating for mental health clinicians to incorporate the role of spirituality into behavioral health approaches, particularly for the treatment of depression.

The path forward does not require us to agree on a single universal definition of spirituality but rather to recognize it is an essential part of what it means to be human. It's about recasting spirituality as a mechanism to pursue more meaningful work lives. Spirituality provides individuals with a sense of identity, wholeness, satisfaction, joy, contentment, beauty, love, respect, positive attitudes, inner peace and harmony, and purpose and direction in life.[47] Acknowledging the important role spirituality plays in people's sense of who they are in the world and how they are connected to a larger whole frames discussions about spirituality as a way to build a shared understanding of our diverse perspectives, values, and beliefs.

As I've delved into the research on how experts have defined and measured "spirituality," I have found it more useful to identify the most mentioned elements in those definitions and measurement tools. These elements are identified below and described in detail in later chapters.

Elements of Spiritual Well-Being

Common themes across many published definitions of spirituality fall into three areas or groups, including the following:

1. Sense of meaning or purpose in life

2. Feeling of connection with others and belonging

3. Connection to transcendence or something universal that is greater than oneself

The definition that was used by the International Spirit at Work awards selection committee when it was actively recognizing companies for addressing spirituality in the workplace succinctly combines these three elements into a working definition.

"Spirituality is the state or experience that can provide individuals with direction or meaning, or provide feelings of understanding, support, inner wholeness or connectedness. Connectedness can be to themselves, other people, nature, the universe, a god, or some other supernatural power. This includes the vertical or transcendent component representing the desire to transcend the individual ego or personality self and the horizontal or service component representing the desire to be of service to other humans and the planet."[48]

As we consider this definition of spirituality and the three areas identified above, we can acknowledge that for some people, interacting with elements of workplace spirituality will likely include some reference to the divine or a specific faith tradition. According to the work of The Fetzer Institute, we must also create space for those who do not believe in the presence of the divine or follow a specific faith tradition.

The key to approaching workplace spirituality at work is to acknowledge that discussions about purpose, meaning, what it means to belong, and how to connect to the transcendent must begin with humility and respect for individual differences. Just as organizations began to deepen discussions about social and racial injustice following the death of George Floyd, we can also consider ways to create a safe container and boundaries around how to engage in interfaith dialogues and respect a diversity of worldviews.

Many organizations have realized the business value of creating a culture that fosters authenticity and vulnerability. This includes inviting employees to present their "true selves," more fully share their life experiences with one another, and bring their "whole self" to work. Hubert Joly, former CEO of Best Buy, describes this as ". . . creating space for every individual to contribute and be valued for who they are, as they are, with their unique perspective and experience. This covers gender, race, ethnicity, and sexual orientation . . . as well as cognitive, age, social, and cultural diversity."[49] Why would we not also include discussions about people's deepest beliefs about who they are, what matters most to them, and how they view themselves within the context of the universe? For some, their identity may be grounded in a specific religion, faith, or wisdom tradition. If we can create inclusive, safe, and authentic discussions about other aspects of diversity, why would we not also extend that to include spirituality? Research shows that when employees are able to express their true selves at work, it is linked with their engagement, job satisfaction, and job performance.[50]

Dr. Judi Neal, the founder of the International Spirit at Work award, asserts there is not likely to ever be a common definition of spirituality because those who define and measure it as part of their research approach it with different perspectives and areas of scholarship. Practical advice for real-world application is to land on the definition that is most appropriate for your context and use of the concept. She goes on to say that discussion about what workplace spirituality means may be more valuable than the final definition an organization decides to use. I agree with the premise that open, respectful dialogue may be a more fruitful path for workplaces than to get hung up on a single universal definition of spirituality.

As you'll see in Part Two of this book, I'll discuss each of the three areas of spirituality identified above as distinct chapters, but addressing spirituality includes all three areas and they are highly inter-related. For example, when talking about one's sense of purpose or meaning in life, individuals often talk about their life roles and relationships. Many life purpose statements mention aspiring to be the best parent, spouse, partner, community member, or friend. We often live out our deepest sense of purpose and values in community with others. Likewise, transcendence is often experienced in the company of others. As the chapter on transcendence discusses, our most profound experiences of awe, wonder, and joy often occur as the result of a deeply felt connection with another person or as part of a group.

My review of the research on spirituality leads me to conclude workplace spirituality is best addressed as a three-legged stool: helping employees have a stronger sense of meaning and purpose for their lives and in their work; a deeper sense of connection and belonging with others; and a connection to something larger than themselves. If you remove any of the legs of the stool, you threaten its ability to support you. Applying this metaphor to workplace spirituality, the strongest approach to support well-being is by addressing all three legs. I separate the conversation about these three elements into separate chapters because it organizes the research about each element and supports discussion about the practical ways organizations can address the elements. But it's important to reinforce this as an artificial separation. Addressing any one of the elements has potential implications for the others, and many practices address all three elements.

Framework for a Comprehensive, Holistic Approach to Workplace Well-Being

In addition to the challenges related to the lack of a consensus definition or measurement approach to workplace spirituality, many corporate initiatives lack a coherent framework or strategic approach to intervention. The following framework attempts to integrate my twenty-five years of experience in the workplace well-being world with my more recent exposure to approaches in the workplace spirituality field. Though I've drawn from models and frameworks proposed in the academic literature, the intent here is to provide practical guidance that ensures an organization's approach is comprehensive enough to yield population-level and organizational-level benefits. Two main organizing parameters are in the proposed well-being framework: levels of influence and dimensions of well-being.

Levels of Influence

When it comes to promoting well-being, it comes down to influencing what we think, say, and do. Each one of us can choose to influence our own well-being but what we think, say, and do also influences those around us. The seminal work of Christakis and Fowler on social networks indicates that our attitudes, beliefs, moods, and behaviors can influence the attitudes, beliefs, moods, and behaviors of those we have direct contact with as well as those we indirectly influence one or two people removed from our primary contacts.[51] Put another way, if you quit smoking, your friends' friends' friends are significantly more likely to quit smoking even if you never met them. If you hold a leadership position or have any type of authority in an organization, your influence holds even more weight because you may be able to change, support, or influence policies, practices, structures, and cultural norms. For this reason, any initiative that endeavors to change what people think, do, and say must address several different levels including individual, interpersonal/group, organizational, and societal. It follows that a comprehensive workplace well-being framework is structured to ensure these four areas are addressed.

The inclusion of the societal level might give you pause, especially if your organization is small, privately held, and doesn't aspire to make a positive impact on the world around it. Even if this is the case, any well-being initiative must consider the significant amount of time that employees spend outside of workplace parameters. Employees live in community with other people, and the places where they live, learn, play, and pray also influence their well-being. For example, access to healthy, affordable food, and safe places to recreate can support healthy eating and physical activity. Advancing community/ societal well-being also supports an organization's employees and their families. Chapter 7 will further detail how organizations can take a multi-level approach to workplace well-being and discuss why it is important to address multiple levels of influence to impact employee well-being at a population level.

Dimensions of Well-Being

The second organizing parameter in the holistic well-being frame-work are the dimensions of well-being you aim to address. The most effective workplace well-being initiatives address multiple dimensions, ideally in an integrated and holistic way that approaches the individual as a whole person rather than as isolated behaviors or conditions. It derives from the understanding that a whole person is made up of interdependent parts, and imbalances in physical, emotional, mental, spiritual, and other aspects of well-being can negatively affect overall well-being. This holistic view was taught by Hippocrates and dates to the 4th century BCE.[52] For example, an individual working on their weight benefits most from approaches that address physical, mental, emotional, social, and spiritual dimensions of well-being. Someone working on more effectively managing burnout and stress would also benefit from approaches addressing these five areas as well as financial well-being (because finances are one of the top stressors for most individuals). In fact, to label any well-being element as addressing only one dimension is counter to the holistic approach. Even so, for planning and communication purposes, workplace well-being practitioners typically group interventions, policies, and approaches into categories based on the primary dimension that appears to be addressed. For example, physical activity supports are grouped in the physical dimension even though physical activity is linked to mental and emotional health.

Most workplace well-being professionals are familiar with the concept of a "well-being wheel," which is a visual representation of both the dimensions of well-being and the levels of influence that an initiative aims to address. One of the most comprehensive well-being wheels in the published literature was developed by Oklahoma State University in 2016.[53]

All four levels of influence are represented along with five dimensions of well-being (physical, emotional, social, spiritual, and professional). Their model is amplified by the inclusion of the populations their well-being initiative aims to serve: employees, students, and community members. It also includes the approaches that are used to address each dimension at each of the four levels of influence.

The number of dimensions an organization aims to address and how they choose to label them is often based on the organization's priorities, population needs, and depth of resources. Moreover, many organizations have codified the different dimensions of well-being into assessment tools for research and program evaluation purposes. For example, the US Centers for Disease Control names six dimensions of well-being (physical, emotional, social, quality of life, life satisfaction, and financial).[54] *Healthy People 2030* names at least ten dimensions, adding the dimensions of purpose/meaning, occupational, intellectual, and spiritual.[55]

Regardless of the number of dimensions selected, the framework and elements of the well-being initiative should be grounded in science demonstrating the effectiveness of each element, coherence of the approach to ensure all stakeholders are aware of and know how to support the elements, and a well-documented strategic plan that ensures all elements are tied to measurable goals and objectives, which are regularly evaluated and improved upon. More information on how to develop an evidence-based, coherent, documented approach for spiritual well-being in the workplace will be addressed in Part Three of this book. But first, Part Two will further illustrate how the spiritual well-being dimension can be addressed at each of the four levels of influence, with special attention on the unique role of leaders, which cuts across all four levels.

CHAPTER 3

HIGHLIGHTS

- Incorporating workplace spirituality into your employee well-being approach does not require you to use spiritual language.

- There is no single consensus definition of workplace spirituality, but three common elements include the following: a sense of meaning and purpose in one's work; a sense of feeling connected, cared for, and belonging at work; and a connection to something larger than oneself. The strongest approach to workplace spirituality incorporates all three elements, and they are strongly inter-related.

- Some scientific evidence shows all human beings have a capacity for spirituality, and eight out of ten people consider themselves to be spiritual to some extent.

- Being spiritual but not religious is possible, yet many people will draw upon a specific faith or wisdom tradition when talking about their source of purpose, the identity they have in the world, and to which groups they feel most connected. We must make space for such authentic conversations when we talk about spirituality.

- Effective spiritual well-being initiatives address employee well-being across four levels of influence including individual, interpersonal, organizational, and social. They also pay special attention to the role of leaders at all levels because they operate at all four levels of influence.

- Effective well-being initiatives address employee well-being in a holistic way across many different dimensions, including physical, mental, emotional, spiritual, financial, and other dimensions.

PART TWO

An Evidence-Based Approach

A Culture of Individual Purpose

"Life is never made unbearable by circumstances,
but only by lack of meaning and purpose."

— VIKTOR FRANKL

Diagnosing Dissonance

*I enter the elegant restaurant and take in the modern but welcoming
space. The large, open floor plan is flooded with golden California sunlight, which reflects off the natural hardwood furniture that is simply
designed but obviously made with care. Small bud vases on the tables
feature the bright orange California poppy, which has set the moun-
tainside meadows ablaze with color. The host greets me and finds me
a table for one, overlooking the property vineyards, olive orchards, and
hiking trails. I pick up the menu, delighted to see the farm-to-table
offerings, which will make it easy for me to stick to my healthy eating
plan of grilled fish and garden vegetables. Under other circumstances,
I would be melting into my chair, savoring every detail, and reveling
in the thought of four days at this luxury resort. So why is my stomach
so twisted in knots? Why is my heart racing in my chest? I try to take in*

some deep calming breaths, but I can't seem to expand my lungs beyond small gulps of air. What is going on?

My visit to the resort is an all-expenses paid leadership training retreat that my boss approved as an investment in my professional development and as a reward for exceeding my department's key performance metrics last year. I'd mentioned the training to my boss during my performance review when he asked me about my professional development goals. I'd been working with one of the co-founders of the Human Performance Institute[56] training program on a collaborative measurement project and was intrigued by its inclusion of spirituality as a component of their training. My boss told me about his approval of the training in the same meeting as he'd shared the news of his departure from the organization. He'd been expecting his release from the company on the heels of the latest organizational change. After talking with several senior leaders, I still didn't know what to call the latest tectonic shift in the organization's infrastructure. Was it a merger or a hostile takeover? I couldn't get a straight answer from anyone, but it resulted in a full executive leadership change. Though the change meant I'd need to deal with educating and building trust with yet another new boss, there was something deeper causing this rare bout of anxiety.

The waiter arrived to take my order and I stuck to my plan, ordering the daily grilled fish and vegetables, then at the last minute adding a glass of white wine to my order. I had been trying to limit my intake of wine as a coping mechanism for work-related stress as part of a faith-based weight management program that I was doing on my own. My work often required me to travel for business, and my colleagues knew I enjoyed wine, so it raised eyebrows when I turned down wine at dinner during previous business trips earlier that month. The rigors of frequent flights back and forth from my home in California to my company's headquar-

ters in Minnesota made following my weight management program more difficult, especially because I didn't feel comfortable talking about the program with my colleagues. I had been looking forward to a week of clean eating, restorative sleep, and long hikes around the property. I told myself that it was just this one glass to help me relax before things kicked off tomorrow, and I'd eliminate wine for the remainder of my time here.

As I waited for my meal to arrive, I pulled out my journal to work through my emotions and discern what had me so wound up. When I was flying back from my latest series of business meetings last week, I had been counting down the days to this retreat. I experienced my first flutter of anxiety as I was unpacking and repacking my bags over the weekend. The retreat center was about ninety minutes from my home, and my anxiety grew with each mile as I drew nearer to the resort. I journaled my way through the possible list of reasons for being nervous about the next few days and got a strong surge of inner affirmation when I named the 360-degree assessment that I'd completed in the weeks leading up to the retreat. I'd received the results on Friday and had scanned them on my long flight home from the East Coast client meeting. The retreat coordinators specified that I have close family members, friends, someone in leadership above me at work, and direct reports from my team complete the pre-retreat assessment. In nearly all cases, the report revealed that my behaviors at work, at home, and in my social circles did not align with the values that I said were most important to me in the survey that I'd completed about myself.

I knew from my conversations with Jack Groppel, one of the founders of this program, that this was a common finding, and the program was intended to help leaders better align their lives with their core values. Professional peers who had been through the program claimed it was a transformational experience. My anxiety came from the sudden reali-zation that it was time to face the truth about the lack of alignment between my core beliefs and my behaviors, and that something in my life had to change in a major way. For example, even though I wasn't attend-ing a church, I still counted my faith as a core part of my identity, but I didn't feel like I could express that part of my identity in my professional life. Deep down, I knew my propensity to swear and drink more heavily around certain people was counter to who I believed I was, and a key ele-ment of this training included facing this hard truth. I wrote a pep talk to myself in my journal, affirming this was something I knew was part of the program and that I'd mentioned the training program to my boss because I knew deep down this was inner work I had to do. Of course, I didn't mention the spiritual well-being component to the training, which branded itself as a leadership performance training. I concluded I might as well try to be open to whatever surfaces over the next few days and work through the implications. In the end, any changes I made because of the training would be choices I decided to make.

The next few days were a combination of classroom-style teaching, break-out conversations with our assigned cohort groups, one-on-one coaching, and hours of self-reflective journal exercises. The primary aim of the first two days was to identify a purpose statement for our lives and prioritize our core values. Based on our purpose and core values, we developed a storyline that detailed the current way we lived our lives against them, and then crafted a desired future story that we envisioned for ourselves. Using the results of the 360-degree assessment, we detailed what specific behaviors needed to change in every aspect of our lives to support our purpose and align our behaviors with our values. From there, we created a ninety-day plan for how we'd embed new or replacement behaviors and practices into our lives and identified accountability partners with whom we could share our intentions.

That retreat happened seven years ago and as I look back through my journals, I see how it was a game changer in terms of my overall spiritual well-being. Before the training, I continued to struggle with work-life balance and occasionally felt burned out and disengaged at work. I knew how to live a healthy lifestyle but often as a coping mechanism, I turned to overconsumption of comfort food, wine, shopping, television, or exotic vacations overseas. It took several years for me to bridge the gap between the "current story" and the "future best-self story" that I journaled about at the retreat, but today I see this exercise was the catalyst to change. In the years since, I've continued to pay attention to my purpose and values, revisiting and refining them and reflecting regularly on the extent to which my lifestyle and leadership aligns to them. I've transitioned from a focus on ego-oriented achievement goals to "be" goals that focus more on how I want to show up in the world. This work of identifying one's purpose represents the first major element of workplace spirituality.

First Workplace Spirituality Element: Fostering a Culture of Purpose and Meaning

Having a life purpose is about having a strong sense of direction for one's life. At its most basic level, it helps us answer life's big questions: "Why am I here?", "What am I living for?", and "What matters most to me?" At a higher, more-developed level, it identifies what in the world breaks your heart and activates you to take action; it draws upon your innate gifts, talents, and strengths to contribute to your well-being and that of others; it is operationalized through activities that engage you in such a way that you fully immerse yourself in what you are doing; and it represents your most enduring principles and values.[57]

Living a purposeful life adds meaning to our everyday moments. Even the dullest tasks can be meaningful. When I was working with a large manufacturing organization years ago, an employee working on the medical tape manufacturing line said she tried to think about how the tape would be used to promote healing for others and it inspired her to do her best at her job. That's what a strong sense of purpose adds to one's life. It makes the mundane more magical and the tedious more transcendent. Life viewed through the lens of purpose can be more fulfilling and satisfying because it contributes to hope for the future and can help us overcome big and small challenges to resilience. The growing research on the importance of life purpose and the challenges facing the world today has moved conversations about purpose into mainstream media, and this critical element of workplace spirituality is often the focus for workplace well-being models that don't specifically name the spiritual well-being domain in their holistic approach. In other words, instead of labeling a segment of their well-being wheel as "spiritual," they label it as "purpose and meaning."

Given that those with a strong sense of purpose experience more meaning and fulfillment, it's no surprise that purpose is linked to happiness. Positive psychology researchers often talk about two pathways to happiness: the hedonic and the eudemonic. The hedonic pathway is associated with pleasure-seeking behaviors, living an enjoyable life, doing what feels good, and taking care of one's needs. Hedonic purpose pathways focus on self-enhancing goals. The eudemonic pathway is associated with living in accordance with one's truest self, aligning with one's deepest values, contributing to others' needs, and striving to reach one's fullest potential. Eudemonic purpose pathways focus on self-transcendent goals.[58] There is ongoing controversy among researchers about how these different pathways contribute to specific aspects of spiritual well-being and life satisfaction, but there seems to be agreement that both aspects are important, and they are complementary or highly related to one another.

Dr. Victor J. Strecher's book, *Life on Purpose*, talks about purpose as having "a higher-order goal that has deep value" and outlines strategies for developing a personal purpose statement.[59] His was one of the first books I picked up to help me go deeper into defining my own purpose after the Human Performance Institute training. Life purpose statements are often aspirational and may not be attainable in one's lifetime. Our life purpose might be broad and work itself out differently across the different life roles that we have. We may develop different purpose statements for different roles in our lives, and we need to keep them in balance because an overemphasis on career purpose and goals can diminish attention to family, friend, community, and personal purpose. Strecher suggests we set limits or boundaries that allow us to direct our energy and attention to our multiple purposes and to create connections between purposes. For example, participating in a work-sponsored community volunteer program may serve a career purpose and a community involvement purpose. Involving one's family and friends in that volunteerism may also contribute to relational purpose. The more we can align and integrate our multiple purposes, the less strain we feel making tradeoffs to balance them.

When it comes to identifying our life purpose, it can be helpful to think about our legacy and how we want to be remembered by others. For example, if you aspire to act with compassion and kindness toward others, your purpose statement might be, "My purpose in life is to act with compassion and kindness by considering others' needs before my own." It helps to think about what matters most in life and how that reflects our deepest values. If family is a top value and you strive to achieve a healthier work-life balance, your purpose statement might be, "My purpose in life is to be a supportive mother and partner, so I prioritize and protect family time on evenings and weekends."

Creating a specific life purpose statement is unnecessary to reap the many benefits linked to a strong life purpose, but articulating what you care most deeply about and why can help. The research linking a strong sense of purpose with well-being focuses on the extent to which individuals say they have a strong sense of purpose for their lives. As you consider what matters most to you, an image may come to mind or a relationship. Certain words or phrases may surface. The key is to identify what they are for you and to intentionally point your energy toward living that purpose in your daily life.

As I think back to the burnout, exhaustion, and lack of fulfillment I experienced earlier in my research career, I realize I had lost my focus on the broader meaning of my work (e.g., helping practitioners and employers understand how to develop effective workplace well-being programs), and I wondered why I pushed myself so hard. It was a question my family and friends often asked, as they were less impressed with scientific journal publications and more interested in my well-being. What I know now but didn't know when I was feeling burned out and dissatisfied with my life was that I needed to get back in touch with my purpose and that it often evolves as we get older.[60] I also needed to re-prioritize self-care because even the most passionate and purposeful people get burned out with lack of adequate rest, proactive recovery periods, and self-care.

Link to Well-Being

Having a strong sense of meaning and purpose is an element in every definition of spirituality that I've encountered but it also contributes to other aspects of well-being. Research demonstrates a reciprocal relationship among purpose, energy, willpower, and health behaviors. The process of aligning yourself with your life purpose takes effort, which requires energy and willpower. But once you align with your purpose, it gives back by energizing you and increasing willpower.[61] Research on willpower has shown that when we connect with our values and purpose using a process called values affirmation, it can bolster our willpower. In one experiment, researchers introduced challenges to study participants' willpower and then studied their eating habits following the introduction of the challenge. When a values affirmation exercise was introduced (e.g., a journaling exercise about their purpose and values), the study participants ate fewer unhealthy foods compared to a control intervention (e.g., a journaling exercise about one's daily routine).[62] According to this research, if you were to pause right now and reflect, talk, or write about your most strongly held values, meaning what matters most to you, it would have a positive influence on your overall well-being.

Our health behaviors also play a role in enhancing our ability to live out our purpose in life. For example, a longitudinal study of more than 14,000 adults over four years showed that individuals with a stronger sense of life purpose at the start of the study were more likely to be more physically active at the end of the study. Likewise, those with higher levels of physical activity at the study's start were more likely to have a strong sense of purpose later in life. This was after controlling for baseline levels of physical activity and purpose.[63] When we get good sleep, practice presence, exercise, eat healthy, and pursue creativity, these behaviors also energize us and contribute to our willpower.[64] In this way, purpose helps fuel the behaviors we desire, and as we repeat those behaviors, they create the energy and willpower required to pursue a purposeful life.

Because individuals with a stronger sense of life purpose are more likely to practice healthy behaviors, a link between purpose and health outcomes exists. One study assessed life purpose and a variety of health behaviors and health outcomes. Over an eight-year period, more than 13,000 US adults were assessed up to five times. When compared to those with the lowest levels of life purpose, adults with the highest sense of purpose were less likely to become physically inactive, develop sleep problems, or gain weight.[65] A different study tracked more than 7,000 adults over six years, finding those with a stronger life purpose at the start of the study were more likely to get subsequent preventive screening exams. Each unit increased in life purpose predicted 17% fewer nights in the hospital.[66]

Researchers at Washington University-St. Louis are studying additional links between purpose and well-being in the Purpose, Aging, Transitions, and Health (PATH) lab. Using a variety of study methodologies across a diversity of geographic locations, age, and population type, the PATH lab is consistently finding a link between having a strong sense of purpose and individual health and well-being. In fact, the current director of the lab, Dr. Patrick Hill, can recall only a couple of times where their PATH lab team hasn't found a positive link between a sense of purpose and one of the outcomes they are studying.[67] Likewise, the Center for Healthy Minds at the University of Wisconsin-Madison has found links among life purpose and memory, cognitive abilities, and lower risk of chronic health conditions such as heart disease or stroke.[68]

Other research links meaningful work to higher levels of psychological well-being and resilience.[69] A more recent prospective Harvard study found that US adults with higher levels of life purpose at baseline were more likely to have better subsequent physical health, healthy lifestyle behaviors, and psychosocial health during a four-year follow-up period.[70]

When Dr. Victor J. Strecher presents a summary of research on the many benefits associated with having a strong purpose, he jokes that if the beneficial effects could be made into a pill, it would be a best-selling drug. The good news is that developing a stronger sense of purpose is free. People willing to invest some time and reflection can strengthen their sense of purpose. I'll be sharing more ideas about how workplace well-being practitioners can incorporate purpose into their well-being initiatives later in this chapter. But wait, there's more! In addition to the many positive impacts of purpose on individual well-being, there are also benefits for the workplace.

Link to Business Outcomes

Research shows that purpose is important for business outcomes as well. A fifteen-year study followed the stock performance of twenty-eight companies (labeled as "Firms of Endearment") that had a corporate purpose that transcended financial goals. These companies were compared against a group of companies focused on their ability to make sound managerial and financial decisions (labeled as "Good to Great companies") and against the Standard & Poor's 500 Index. Though the Good to Great companies had the best financial performance in the first three years of the study, the Firms of Endearment companies had much stronger financial returns over the length of the study, returning 1,681% of the initial investment by the end of the study.[71] What might contribute to such resounding financial returns?

Researchers have linked purpose-driven organizations with higher levels of employee engagement with their work, attraction and retention of talent, job satisfaction, worker productivity, and customer loyalty, all of which contribute to corporate financial performance.[72] Purpose-driven organizations are those that prioritize contributing to the greater good of society over the mere focus on financial profitability. The purpose is clearly articulated and incorporated into every aspect of corporate decision making and business operations.[73]

There are also links between individual purpose and related outcomes. Researchers demonstrate that individuals who report living out their life purpose at work are more likely to report higher engagement levels.[74] Gallup research has also demonstrated a link between employees having a strong sense of purpose and employee engagement, which can also lead to higher customer ratings, increased productivity and quality, lower turnover, and less absenteeism.[75]

In 2017, researchers at BetterUp Labs conducted a survey of more than 2,200 US employees across twenty-six industries.[76] They found that employees with a strong sense of purpose were more likely to find meaning in their work and those who rated their work as very meaningful reported 51% greater job satisfaction than employees who reported finding the least amount of meaning in their work. They are also more likely to work longer work weeks and are absent less. The resulting gains in worker productivity add up to over $9,000 per worker per year.

There is also a strong link between employees' purpose and their likelihood to remain with their organization. A 2021 nationally representative poll of US workers found that purpose-driven employees are more likely to stay with their company for two or more years and are also more engaged with their work.[77] Of the 7,000 global employees surveyed in August of 2021 by Edelman Trust Barometer, 59% were seeking to change their jobs primarily because they wanted a job they felt was a better fit with their values. Employees who felt their values and beliefs were aligned with the company they work for were more likely to say they would keep working for their organization for many years (76%) compared to their peers who were not purpose-driven (63%).[78]

Purpose is even more powerful when combined with the second workplace spirituality element of connection, which will be discussed in the next chapter. Researchers found average turnover risk is reduced by 24% for companies whose employees report strong levels of social support and shared purpose.[79]

Researchers from McKinsey & Company have shown that employees who say they are living out their purpose at work experience higher levels of work effectiveness and four times higher engagement with their work, and yet only one-third of study participants believed their organizations supported them in living out their purpose at work.[80]

Are you convinced that incorporating the workplace spirituality element of purpose is a worthwhile consideration as part of your organization's well-being initiatives? If so, keep reading to learn how you can apply this research in practical ways within the world of work.

Application to Practice

Given these many benefits, it behooves organizations to incorporate the workplace spirituality element of purpose-alignment into the employee experience. The workplace could offer many vehicles for supporting employees in purpose-development and skill building around managing and living a purposeful life. Peele suggests a phased approach that incorporates purpose into executive leadership training and then offering training to front-line managers and supervisors, and then to the broader employee population. Employers should also look for opportunities to weave purpose and values into onboarding and diversity, equity, and inclusion (DEI) efforts.[81] At least three studies support a link between strong life purpose and comfort with ethnic diversity among White adults, which might be of interest to your DEI colleagues.[82]

Given the strong connection to meaningful work, purpose-development can be incorporated into employee well-being initiatives and into career development activities. This includes offering self-paced learning modules or tools that guide employees in thinking about their life purpose, incorporating purpose activities into employee mentorship and coaching, and teaching managers and supervisors to role model and support employees in purpose-development and purpose-alignment in their work. Likewise, team building activities can incorporate purpose by guiding team members through a series of reflections and discussions around the identification of team-based values and goals. Teams can create their own purpose and value statements, with self-managed teams creating mechanisms for accountability and support.

Programs have been developed to support organizations in the design and implementation of purpose development initiatives within their organizations. The focus is on addressing employee purpose and helping employees to identify for themselves how their purpose applies to their work and home lives.[83] Journal reflections, meditation practices, and self-assessment tools are often incorporated into purpose-development activities. Self-reflection and contemplative practices provide significant support to development of a purpose statement because they help individuals get in touch with what is important to them and what they value most. Some organizations offer individual and group coaching as well as individual and group training. Unity Lab has developed a scalable peer group model that is optimized to promote diversity, build purposeful teams, and foster a deeper sense of belonging at work.[84]

My foray into purpose development at work began with the Human Performance Institute leadership retreat I described in the opening story to this chapter[85], and leaders have a special role to play in supporting a purpose-driven culture.[86] A purpose-driven culture is one where employees understand how their individual and team roles contribute to the overall mission of the company. It includes the promotion of the values and purpose of the broader organization and the attention to how individual purpose statements align with it. Employees and leaders at all levels of an organization are held accountable to living the organization's purpose and values, but a purpose-driven organization also aims to help employees align their life purpose to their work. Most importantly, purpose and values take center stage to guide leadership and organizational decision making. Metrics can be developed to measure the extent to which employees and teams perceive their personal purpose aligns with the organization's purpose and to measure the extent to which direct reports perceive their leaders as living out their purpose and values.

Some specific actions that leaders can take to support employees and teams in pursuing their purpose include incorporating purpose into corporate and team communications, creating opportunities for employees to share their stories of how they are living out their purpose, and including employees at all levels in defining or revisiting the organization's purpose.[87] As reflected in the employer examples that follow, senior leaders can set the tone for a purpose-driven culture by establishing an organizational purpose that seeks to make the world a better place as part of its business model. Mid-level managers and supervisors are in a better position to work with individual employees to help them identify their specific life purpose and discuss how it might align with the organization's larger purpose. The Best Buy example below is a good demonstration of this approach.

Some suggest that purpose is a journey and a practice rather than a destination. It evolves over time and must be revisited and updated, especially during times of transition or change. In our teenage years, purpose is often associated with one's skills or interests, but most people develop a greater sense of purpose during their twenties and thirties. Building a career, starting a family, making choices about faith or religious practices, and volunteerism experiences can contribute to a sense of purpose. During midlife, one's sense of purpose and focus can shift as individual identities related to work and family life change. A 2021 study found purpose can diminish in midlife but those who can maintain a strong sense of purpose through midlife had better health over time.[88] Emerging health issues can also influence energy levels and physical functioning, which is tied to the kinds of activities in which we engage.[89] Understanding that purpose and values can change for individuals over time requires that programs and resources are consistently available to support employees in evolving their personal purpose statements over time. Linking these efforts to discussions about career development and growth can be especially powerful as employees who have been with an organization for several years might be looking for new opportunities, and revisiting their purpose and values can help them identify new roles or challenges that keep them engaged with the organization. The employer examples that follow demonstrate how some organizations have incorporated the workplace spirituality element of employee purpose into their operations.

Employer Examples

Numerous examples of employers pursuing purpose at an organizational level focus on the organization's reason for being in the world and how employees within the organization are positioned to make a positive impact. Organizations like Southwest Airlines and Patagonia are often referenced as role models, inspiring other organizations to follow suit.[90] The key is not to stop at the organizational level, assuming the company mission and value statements will translate into a meaningful work experience and a thriving culture for all employees. Attention must also be paid to the individual employee's personal purpose, positioning the organization as one potential vehicle for the broader contributions an employee might make in their world, but recognizing that it may not be the only mechanism for positive impact. Rey and colleagues suggest in *Purpose-Driven Organizations* that individual purpose must be activated for an organization to reap the full benefits of becoming a purpose-driven organization.[91] The following organizations have taken a robust approach to cultivating a purpose-driven culture that includes addressing employee purpose.

Best Buy

Best Buy is a consumer electronics retail company with about 100,000 employees in the United States and Canada. The fifty-five-year-old, multinational company is publicly traded and was named in Barron's as the "most sustainable company in America" in 2019 and 2021.[92] Although the purpose-driven company was considered an "essential" business by pandemic standards in many states, the company decided to close its doors to customers at the start of the global pandemic out of concern for employee health and safety. The entire chain shifted its nearly 1,000 stores to an online business in forty-eight hours and then temporarily suspended in-home deliveries and installations until more information regarding COVID-19 became available.[93]

As the pandemic lingered on, Best Buy strengthened its approach to customer service by quickly establishing contact-free curbside pick-up and expanding existing in-home consultation capabilities to include online, chat, and phone technology consultations. Best Buy also paid all store employees for a full month following the temporary closure of stores, paid hourly appreciation pay for frontline workers, and established hardship funds for employees in need. The company enhanced mental health, childcare, and caregiver benefits and increased the minimum wage to $15 an hour.

The remarkable year-over-year financial earnings reported by Best Buy over the past five years (2017–2021) represents a sea change from its status in 2012, when the company was considered by many to be on the brink of extinction. At that time, Best Buy hired Hubert Joly to spearhead a turnaround, and under his leadership, the company transformed its approach to profitability by focusing first on its employees. Best Buy's turnaround story is described in detail in Joly's book *The Heart of Business* and emphasizes a purpose-driven culture with operations that foster rich human connections between employees as well as between employees and customers.[94]

One of the early efforts in the six-year turnaround journey was to identify a "noble purpose" for Best Buy. Through a series of discovery workshops with leaders at all levels, Best Buy's noble purpose became "to enrich our customers' lives through technology." The next step was to engage all employees in identifying their individual purpose and work with them to align that with Best Buy's noble purpose. This effort began with a series of workshops involving leaders who knew the company best. From these workshops, a concept emerged that positioned every Best Buy sales associate as ". . . an inspiring friend who helps customers understand what they want to do and imagine how technology can help them." Expanding on this concept, the associates defined what it meant to be an inspiring friend and how that person would behave to deliver on that promise. To clarify what this meant in practice, Best Buy rolled out more workshops with employees across all its US stores. Everyone in the company was expected to participate, even members of the board of directors. This concise summary of Best Buy's phased approach sounds straightforward, but it took many months to coordinate, implement, and follow through on the discoveries made from each of the workshops. It was a substantial discovery exercise that incorporated personal storytelling and facilitation to help the noble purpose and the vision of employees serving as an inspiring friend to emerge.

With the noble purpose identified, the concept of the inspired friend defined and described, and specific behaviors identified through subsequent employee workshops, the next challenge was operationalizing the behaviors and infusing them into all business operations. Best Buy held a Holiday Leadership Meeting, which gathered together store managers from all over the United States for two to three days. A stage was installed at the center of the room and the agenda began with frontline employees and managers sharing personal stories about what inspired them. The stories allowed employees at all levels to deepen their relationships with one another and consider how they could work together to help all employees on their team fulfill their individual purpose in life through their work at Best Buy. The annual gathering also featured a charitable activity (building computers for disadvantaged kids), as a reminder of the human-focus of the company's noble purpose. Annual meetings like this continued, and managers were trained to support employees in aligning their individual purpose to their work within Best Buy. For example, one district manager learned that one of his direct reports aspired to move out of her parents' house and live independently in her own apartment. Over several years, the manager worked with her to develop her leadership and supervisory skills until she was able to move into a leadership role within Best Buy. Her team members cheered her on and celebrated the realization of her dream when she was promoted.

Eventually, Best Buy developed measurement tools to track how well purpose was embedded into company practices. The company's people-first culture emphasized metrics focused on employee turnover, employee engagement rates, and ensuring performance appraisals were conducted regularly and on time. It also influenced hiring practices as the specific behaviors and attributes of "being an inspiring friend" were clarified and operationalized.

Best Buy's journey from financially struggling to thriving was built through an iterative process: It emphasized a people-first philosophy; framed the company's noble purpose in a meaningful, human, authentic way; explored what drove the people within each team; identified and celebrated meaningful moments that mattered by sharing stories; and encouraged role modeling from leaders at all levels. Annual Holiday Leadership Meetings continued year-over-year, with the 2019 meeting theme "I Am Best Buy" focusing on how each individual's story contributes to the fabric of the company. Operating under Joly's people-centric principles, Best Buy's share price went from about $11 a share in fall of 2012 to $75 a share by June of 2019 and recorded six straight years of growth. He credits this success to employees at all levels embracing the shift to a purpose-driven, people-centric culture, and it's that transition that he emphasizes throughout his telling of Best Buy's turnaround story. According to Joly, the financial success merely affirmed that if you focus on people first, profitability will follow.

ProMedica

ProMedica is an integrated, non-profit health care organization that has experienced massive growth over the past few years, tripling the size of its workforce from 15,000 in 2018 to more than 55,000 and expanding from service in six states to twenty-eight states. As the organization worked to unify across its much larger enterprise, the CEO incorporated employee purpose into its alignment and rebranding initiatives.

ProMedica CEO Randy Oostra explains, "Anytime an organization grows through acquisition, building a common culture is paramount. Focusing on purpose gives us a platform that conveys to our employees the importance our organization places on—just the work they do. It's also an important way to align our leaders from a values perspective."[95]

This immediately elevated the strategic importance of employee purpose and well-being as a driver of organizational success. ProMedica relied on a tiered approach to implementation, beginning with company leadership. More than 100 leaders were led through the development of their own purpose statements and a sampling of these were shared with an initial group of 6,000 employees as part of a video. These early adopters were led through a process of detailing purpose-fueled commitments in a mobile app developed by Kumanu called "Purposeful Leader Quest." Subsequent efforts infused purpose into supporting content and materials, which were delivered through internal channels and ProMedica's well-being ambassadors. Monthly themed content was incorporated into presentation slides, blog posts, facility signage, and various internal delivery channels. Purpose Challenges, PurposeCasts with Kumanu CEO Victor J. Strecher, onboarding webinars, and livestreams were also developed in an ongoing partnership between ProMedica and Kumanu.

Due to robust executive leadership support, employee engagement in the purpose initiative was strong, and results from the first phase of rollout exceeded leadership expectations. Employees who reported a low sense of purpose and feelings of anxiety, depression, or elevated risk for burnout at the start of the initiative improved in all areas over the next sixty days. Nearly half (46%) reported reductions in anxiety, 44% reduced depressive symptoms, 38% improved in sense of purpose, and 29% reduced burnout symptoms. A 54% improvement in engagement at work was also observed. Even more exceptional was the timing of these improvements: in the midst of one of the heaviest waves of the COVID-19 hospitalizations for their health system.

Both organizations featured in these employer examples addressed many aspects of employee well-being prior to expanding their focus to include life purpose. They are also similar in that they rolled out purpose-driven activities in an iterative fashion, which included engaging leaders at all levels of the organization from executives to frontline managers. What differs is how these companies positioned and framed their efforts. Though ProMedica incorporated purpose into an enterprise-wide strategic rebranding initiative, Best Buy eventually infused purpose into how it does business. Promedica's purpose initiative was launched more recently, so time will tell how sustainable and impactful its efforts will be.

In these examples, addressing life purpose was not limited to a short-term campaign or a single programmatic offering. In both organizations, discussions about purpose were woven into the fabric of the organization and helped employees understand that attention to one's purpose and values are strongly linked to overall well-being and thriving at work as well as to business performance. In the next chapter, we will address the element of relationships, which is strongly tied to purpose because our relationships tend to be the first thing we think of when asked, "What matters most to you in life?"

CHAPTER 4

HIGHLIGHTS

- Individuals with a strong sense of purpose tend to live longer, healthier lives, have higher levels of well-being, and be more engaged with their work. Employees with a strong sense of purpose are more likely to find their work meaningful, to be more engaged with their work, to be more strongly connected with co-workers, and to be more productive and more likely to remain with their organization.

- Purpose-driven organizations prioritize contributing to the greater good of society over the relentless pursuit of financial profitability and incorporate their purpose into corporate decision-making and business operations. Activating organizational purpose requires helping individual employees to identify their life purpose and consider how their work allows them to live out their purpose.

- Employers can help employees identify meaning and purpose in their work and in their lives by embedding it into many facets of their work. Practical steps include the following:

  o Engage executive level leaders in identifying their individual purpose before engaging the rest of the organization

  o Incorporate purpose discussions into team building activities and guide team members to create a purpose statement and values for their team

- o Work with managers to help them incorporate individual purpose into performance and professional development conversations with their direct reports

- o Incorporate reflections about purpose into well-being classes, webinars, and individual coaching

- o Offer peer group discussions that allow diverse groups of employees to discuss their source of meaning, purpose, and values with one another in an authentic, non-judgmental way

- o Incorporate reflections about purpose and individual storytelling about what matters most to employees into annual strategy planning meetings and retreats

- o Add measures of individual purpose and perceptions about opportunities to live out one's purpose at work into employee pulse surveys and engagement surveys

CHAPTER 5

A Culture of Connection and Belonging

"Connection is the energy that is created between people when they feel seen, heard, and valued; when they can give and receive without judgment. Belonging is the innate human desire to be part of something larger than us."

— BRENÉ BROWN

From Outcomes-Driven to Relationship-Driven Work

The year is 1997. I am two years into my first professional job in the workplace wellness field and I'm sitting through a performance review with my supervisor. I work hard and meet all my project deadlines, so I am expecting a favorable performance review. My supervisor recognizes my reliability in completing my assigned tasks and expresses appreciation for the extra projects I've taken on in the past year. I beam with pride as he shares some positive feedback.

"Overall, you work hard and the others on the team know they can depend on you to get your work done. They feel more comfortable work-

ing with you compared to in the past and say you seem more relaxed and friendly. You've contributed to some solid quality improvement projects this past year and did a great job of coordinating the new classes we offered."

But things take an unexpected turn when we get to the portion of the review focused on professional improvement. Clearing his throat, my supervisor continues, "When it comes to doing your assigned job and completing tasks, you are doing terrific. But outcomes are not the only thing that matter. The thing you need to focus on for the year ahead is how you go about executing your work. Based on the 360-degree feedback surveys, the team says you come off as intimidating and controlling. When things don't go according to plan, you appear to get frustrated and irritable. You are impatient. When I am not around, they feel you are bossy and overpowering."

As my supervisor reads through the feedback, I feel my heart pounding in my chest and tension bubbling up within me. It begins as a clenched stomach, progresses up through my ribcage, and ends as a tight ball in my throat. I sweat as I try to maintain an appearance of professional poise. Feeling as though I am under attack, I bristle in defense. How can my co-workers feel this way about me? I always show up early and stay late. I complete my work on time. I try to take a team approach and when I appear to be taking over their work, it's because my work is done, and they are always behind. I'm doing them a favor by picking up their slack to keep the center running well. I'm trying to be helpful. If it wasn't for me, a lot of things wouldn't get done on time. Where is the gratitude? But I leave this unsaid, inwardly seething.

My supervisor lays down the piece of paper he's been reading and looks up, removing his reading glasses. "Look, I know this feedback is hard to take but I have to say I agree with the team on much of this. Overall, you are completing your job responsibilities well, but you do *need to work on how you execute. Would you be open to developing a more team-oriented approach over the next year?"*

My mouth is so dry I can hardly respond, and I take a sip of water from my water bottle as I try to formulate a reply. I suddenly realize that I've been holding my breath and take a deep inhale and exhale, letting my shoulders drop a few inches away from the position they've taken near my ears.

Fighting back the urge to cry, I decide to be honest with my boss. I try to keep my tone even and avoid the appearance of being defensive. "I have to say, I'm surprised to hear my co-workers feel this way. I am not trying to be intimidating or controlling." I hear my voice trembling with emotion and take another sip of water, trying to calm myself. Taking another deep breath to steady myself, I continue. "When they say I am overstepping and taking control of their work, I'm trying to be helpful because I see they are behind on deadlines for their projects. I thought that by helping them complete their projects, I was taking a team approach. I didn't know I was offending them." I realize I am sounding defensive despite my best efforts and so finish with utter humility. "I feel so embarrassed and want to make things right. Do you think I should say something to my colleagues and apologize? I don't want to be unpleasant to work with. I really care about my job and want to do well." I look down at my hands, too ashamed to look him in the eye.

"That's a step in the right direction to want to change what you are doing. And as I said, you've done an exemplary job of meeting your goals. We need to shift some of that energy from what *you are doing to* how *you're getting the work done."*

My supervisor and I spend the next thirty minutes discussing specific steps I can take to adjust my approach to my work in the year ahead. Knowing I am an avid reader, he recommends a book that I can read to work on a team-oriented approach. And he suggests I look into the free career development courses offered through our employer. I express my desire to increase my hours to full-time work and ask what opportunities might exist for me to take on additional projects, perhaps outside of the fitness center. I've been doing some side projects in the research institute that serves as the umbrella organization for the unit that contractually staffs the fitness center and don't seem to be getting the same kind of feedback in that setting. It's probably because I am given a task I can execute entirely on my own and because I work more autonomously. I'm doing work for a results-oriented person who seems pleased with the pace and quality of my work. Would it be possible to do more projects within that environment because my work style appears to be more conducive to that setting? My supervisor considers this for a moment, and we end the discussion agreeing to a two-pronged approach. He'll inquire into additional opportunities to increase my hours by taking on new projects within the research institute, and I will take my co-workers' feedback to heart, invest in self-paced professional development, and sign up for one of the offered professional development courses. Above all, I need to be less domineering and rigid in my interactions with my co-workers. I need to let go of wanting to control their work and focus on relationship building.

I'm glad we scheduled the review as the last hour of my work shift. I do my best to be warm and friendly and listen more than talk during the brief overlap with a team member coming to relieve me as she begins her shift. I attempt to keep my tone light and my facial expression open and friendly. I ask her about her day, ask if there is anything I can do for her before I leave, and compliment her on her outfit. As I pack up my things and leave, I am relieved to depart the building.

I am thankful for the thirty-minute drive home so I can process the information I received before I go home to dinner with my husband. I decide to do whatever I can to make things right at work while also seeking a new position elsewhere. Clearly, I do not fit with this team. I've known it since I was told by my previous supervisor on her last day (about six months ago) that she almost did not hire me after my internship with the parent organization two years ago. My co-workers did not feel comfortable with me then and it was only because I'd made such a strong impression on my boss's boss that I'd been hired. My feedback at that time was to work on the appearance of being over-confident and even "cocky." She said I appeared to be impatient about letting things work their way through certain hurdles and red tape. Although I impressed people with my professionalism, attention to detail, and thoroughness, it was hard for me to hide my disdain for others who were not as organized or as on top of things as I was. I thought I was addressing those concerns, but clearly, I have a lot of work to do. Feeling connection and a sense of belonging at work is a key aspect of workplace spirituality. As I discovered firsthand, it has implications for job satisfaction, employee engagement, and workplace performance.

In 1992, Dr. Jim Loehr and Dr. Jack Groppel co-founded Johnson & Johnson's Human Performance Institute, which hosted the leadership retreat that I would attend many years later and discussed in the previous chapter. By then, I'd learned through experience that a focus on aggressive over-achievement without the balance of attention to how I got results would negatively influence my relationships at work. The cost of that lopsided focus on an individual level was isolation, loneliness, and a lack of meaningful connection with others. I knew it was a problem but struggled to figure out how to translate that knowledge into sustainable behaviors that would enrich and deepen my relationships at work and in life. It's one thing to know what I wanted to achieve (deeper and more authentic relationships) and another to figure out how to present myself in a way that cultivated better relationships (approach-

able, compassionate, and vulnerable). It also had implications for team performance. My achievement-oriented behavior was often perceived by team members as aggressive and alienating, which negatively impacted team cohesion. This made it less likely that others would seek my input or invite me to collaborate even though I was eager to contribute to broader team outcomes. Nothing in my academic or professional training addressed relationship building at work.

In his recent book, Leading with Character, *Dr. Loehr distinguishes between performance character strengths, which are necessary for high achievement and performance, and moral character strengths, which reflect a value on how we treat others.[96] Performance character strengths include focus, persistence, confidence, and discipline, among others, and moral character strengths include kindness, honesty, compassion, gratitude, and humility, among others. Performance character strengths contribute to high achievement regardless of moral character strengths. As I think back to my performance review with my manager at the start of my career, I was over-reliant on performance character, which drove a focus on what I accomplished, at the expense of moral character, which attended to how I got there. I deeply appreciate my manager pointing this out to me, but I think I missed the opportunity to dig into the root causes contributing to my overvaluing the destination and undervaluing the journey when it came to meeting work deliverables.*

Loehr also discusses Imposter Syndrome as one potential root cause of this imbalance, emphasizing performance over moral character strengths. Though I didn't recognize it at the time, it played a role in my experience of burnout and isolation later in my career. Imposter Syndrome is the belief that one is inadequate or undeserving of one's role or success, which leads to the belief that it's only a matter of time before others figure this out.[97] The fear of being exposed as a fraud feeds feelings of insecurity, causing one to work harder. Sacrifices are made along the way, and one can neglect self-care (e.g., getting rest, eating healthy foods, and fostering quality relationships). Most of us can relate to making tradeoffs between prioritizing work demands over self-care, but it becomes problematic when this occurs over a sustained period. My experience of burnout occurred after years of putting my work and school obligations ahead of my physical, mental, social, and spiritual well-being needs.

The impact on one's relationships goes deeper than a mere neglect of one's social connections. According to Loehr, the self-doubt associated with Imposter Syndrome leads to the following:

> *. . . a lack of trust and confidence in others . . . when we experience self-doubt, we not only judge ourselves critically, but are more likely to judge others critically, which can impact our ability to build strong, healthy, and productive relationships. Additionally, those who struggle with Imposter Syndrome often feel they can never really let people know who they are, because in their mind they are a fraud. This can cause others to perceive them as very distant and difficult to know, which can undermine trust and team spirit.[98]*

What I failed to realize early in my career is the vital importance of my relationships at work on my overall quality of life and well-being. As much as I tried to compartmentalize my life into the "professional me" and the "personal me," what was going on in my relationships at work carried over into my personal life. I felt as if I always needed to keep my guard up, took myself way too seriously, and carefully protected and projected the image I wanted everyone to believe about who I was. In some ways, these behaviors nourished the Imposter Syndrome because every layer of veneer I painted over my most authentic self made expressing the fullness of who I was to others much harder.

Research now tells us that being able to present the fullness of our most authentic selves makes a difference in terms of our contributions at work and in life. Imposter Syndrome kept me from bringing my most authentic self into my work, which negatively impacted my sense of social connectedness and belonging with co-workers. The strong influence that social connection has on the health, well-being, and performance of individuals and teams reinforces the importance of addressing this second element of workplace spirituality.

Second Workplace Spirituality Element: Fostering a Culture of Connection and Belonging

In addition to fostering a culture of purpose and meaning at work, cultivating connection and belonging is an equally critical component of workplace spirituality. Think about it: Full-time employees spend more than half of their waking hours engaged in the workplace environment, including meetings and communications with co-workers. It's no surprise, then, that the nature of our interactions with co-workers and customers has a significant influence on our mental, emotional, and social well-being. Most employees long to feel more authentic connection at work.

Connection has become a bit of a loaded word in modern times because we've never been so highly networked with others while being able to hide our true selves. Digital technology allows us to talk, text, tweet, message, or video chat at the push of a button. Communication strategies abound with the choice of asynchronous or real-time exchanges. Social media platforms enable us to become acquainted with hundreds of thousands of people all over the world and judge the quality of their posts with a thumbs-up or thumbs-down. The world of avatars allows us to present ourselves to others as we'd most like others to see us, with the editing features on our phones or computer cameras ensuring we're angled, lit, and cropped in the most aesthetically pleasing way. Despite the plethora of communication mechanisms available to us and access to anyone with a digital device, we've never been lonelier or felt more disconnected.

A 2019 survey of more than 10,000 US adults, found that 61% of respondents felt lonely, a seven-point increase since the survey was first fielded in 2018.[99] As this was prior to many workers shifting to work-from-home environments in the global pandemic, we might assume the trends have not improved. Researchers base these estimates on a loneliness index score comprised of responses to eleven survey questions, which provide a deeper understanding of the phenomenon. More than half of respondents reported they felt like no one knows them well or they often felt left out. Nearly half felt isolated from others and their relationships with others were not meaningful. More than a third felt other people do not respect their skills and abilities, and about one-quarter of Americans believe no one shares their interests and concerns. Leaders are also highly likely to report a lack of social connection. A 2012 *Harvard Business Review* survey found that half of CEOs reported experiencing feelings of loneliness.[100] In light of this information, it's important to clarify what is meant by creating a culture of connection.

Dr. Brené Brown defines connection as ". . . the energy that exists between people when they feel seen, heard, valued; when they can give and receive without judgment; and when they derive sustenance and strength from the relationship."[101] Loneliness scores tend to improve with the frequency of in-person interactions that people have, but the 2019 Cigna survey found that 83% of respondents said the frequency of their in-person social interactions were less than they desired.

How do workplaces address the second element of workplace spirituality by fostering a rich sense of connection and belonging? One obvious solution might be to host more networking socials and sponsor sports leagues, but work gatherings often don't promote meaningful connection. And there is the additional need to address the innate human desire to feel like one belongs. Poet and philosopher John O' Donohue writes the following:

> . . . belonging is deep; only in a superficial sense does it refer to our external attachment to people, places, and things. It is the living and passionate presence of the soul. Belonging is the heart and warmth of intimacy. When we deny it, we grow cold and empty. Our life's journey is the task of refining our belonging so that it may become more true, loving, good, and free.[102]

Addressing this second element of workplace spirituality goes beyond simply creating more opportunities for employees to interact with one another. There is a qualitative aspect that requires attention to how people feel because of those interactions. Do they feel like valued and respected contributors who are equally and fairly included in workplace operations?

The importance of the quality of one's connections with others is inherent in Brené Brown's definition of connection. Social psychologist and researcher Dr. Julianne Holt-Lunstad studies the link between social connectedness and health. In her research, she refers to social connection as physical, behavioral, cognitive, and emotional, with three major components:

1. Structural support via physical or behavioral presence of others in our lives

2. Functional support via the perception that support is available to us

3. Quality support via the positive or negative emotional nature of our relationships

All three components inform the extent to which we feel high or low levels of social connection; therefore, fostering a culture of connection and belonging requires all three elements be addressed.[103] At work, we may be surrounded by a lot of people in our immediate environment (structural support) but may not perceive that our co-workers care about our struggles, successes, or aspirations outside of our work responsibilities (functional support). If the first two elements are present, but co-workers perceive our interactions to be largely negative (quality support), this can also diminish one's overall sense of connection at work.

As I think back to the time in my career when I felt the most isolated and lonely, I had strong levels of structural and quality but lacked functional support. I believed that my co-workers valued my contributions but did not believe they cared about me as a person. Due to Imposter Syndrome, I was afraid to be fully authentic with people and, therefore, compromised on living out my deepest values in an effort to fit in and be liked. Perhaps this is something you can relate to. As you consider the three components of social connection, how would you rate your immediate team and your organization as a whole? What aspects of support are strong and where is more attention needed to support social connection more fully in the workplace?

Some leaders might feel like attending to social connection is a "nice to have" and might prioritize it below meeting performance goals. The next sections address the importance of social connection and belonging for worker well-being and business outcomes. In their book, *Work Better Together,* co-authors Jen Fisher and Anh Phillips assert that meaningful work relationships are foundational to workplace well-being. Moreover, enjoying work and experiencing the satisfaction of meaningful relationships at work is energizing, with links to employee and team performance.[104]

Link to Well-Being

A well-established link exists between the quality and frequency of our social connections and various aspects of our well-being. A 2006 review examined the physiological mechanisms that help explain the correlation between higher levels of social support and lower rates of mortality and morbidity, finding evidence related to cardiovascular, neuroendocrine, and immune function.[105] Individuals with higher levels of social support are also more likely to take care of themselves through positive self-care behaviors (e.g., smoking cessation and medication adherence)[106] and to report better cognitive functioning,[107] with less depression[108] and greater life satisfaction[109]. In summary, higher levels of social connection are associated with higher levels of physical, mental, and emotional well-being.

There is a separate body of research devoted to observing the health and well-being implications when there is a lack of social connection. As the global pandemic with its requirements to physically distance ourselves contributed to a lack of social connection, it also amplified growing trends related to loneliness, which is a feeling. According to Dr. Jeremy Nobel, a physician and faculty member at Harvard Medical School as well as founder of The Unlonely Project, physical isolation associated with the pandemic especially exacerbated the risk of loneliness for marginalized populations. Any individuals who went into the pandemic uncertain about how other people viewed them or felt a lower sense of regard by others (e.g., people of color, those who identified as being in a minority gender-affiliated group) were at risk for loneliness and this contributed to even greater inequities in health and well-being for these groups.[110]

Research links chronic loneliness with increased likelihood of dementia, cognitive decline, immunity issues, and heart disease, which contributes to a shorter lifespan.[111] When people feel lonelier, they are more sensitive to negative interactions at work, perceiving these interactions to be more stressful. One review found that lonely individuals are more likely to interpret hostile intent, expect rejection, evaluate themselves and their co-workers negatively, and have low self-efficacy.[112] According to Dr. Nobel, those experiencing loneliness tend to have inaccurate judgments about other people's impressions of them and their desire to be connected with them. Lonely individuals may feel they are not interesting enough or worthy enough by other people's standards and so tend to withdraw even more. I can identify with such feelings. When I felt lonely at work in the past, I tended to self-isolate by turning down invitations to go to lunch or out to happy hour socials with co-workers. It was easy for me to blame my workload, saying I needed to work through lunch or stay at the office late to catch up on things. Though that may have been true, I see now that an element of self-isolation was present. Deep down, I felt I couldn't be my authentic self and worried that if people got to know me, they wouldn't think I was interesting enough to invite out again. The relationship between social connection and well-being influences worker productivity and performance, which contributes to business outcomes.

Link to Business Outcomes

There is a strong business case for attending to social connectedness among workers. Among CEOs who report feeling lonely, 61% say it hinders their performance on the job, particularly for first-time CEOs.[113] Lonely workers at all levels are more likely to feel a lack of connection with co-workers and report a lack of belonging at work, which is linked to their commitment to the organization.[114] Other research has found that loneliness for just one member of a team can negatively influence the team's performance because the individual's diminished ability to execute his or her tasks and communicate effectively with others has implications for the whole group.[115] US Surgeon General Vivek Murthy has taken on loneliness as an issue of concern for all citizens based on its link to health and well-being but also mentions the business implications in a *Harvard Business Review* article: "At work, loneliness reduces task performance, limits creativity, and impairs other aspects of executive function such as reasoning and decision making."[116]

On the other end of the spectrum are the positive outcomes linked to high levels of social connection and belonging. A longitudinal study documented what happens when employees report feeling affection, compassion, and caring for others at work on patient and organizational outcomes in a long-term care setting. They found more positive feelings were associated with better patient mood, quality of life, satisfaction, and a decrease in future trips to the emergency room. A positive workplace culture of support is also associated with employee satisfaction and lower rates of absenteeism and emotional exhaustion.[117] Research from BetterUp Labs surveyed more than 1,700 full-time employees across multiple industries and conducted intervention experiments with another 2,000 participants. They found that workers who felt a high sense of belonging at work experienced a 56% increase in job performance, a 50% drop in turnover risk, and a 75% reduction in sick days.[118]

Researchers at the University of Michigan's Center for Positive Organizations have identified and examined the influence of virtuousness in organizations. Virtuousness is manifested as behaviors, processes, and routines that display moral excellence or inherent goodness. Examples include demonstrations of forgiveness, humility, wisdom, and compassion (moral character strengths) in the workplace, all of which are likely to foster a culture of connection and belonging.[119]

One of the Center's studies of eight business units within the same large organization found that business units displaying higher measures of compassion, integrity, forgiveness, trust, and optimism during company-wide downsizing had higher levels of productivity, work quality, profitability, and customer retention and had lower employee turnover. A larger study across sixteen industries examined the same measures of virtuousness among the study sample, which represented organizations that had recently cut staff. Profitability, quality, innovation, employee turnover, and customer retention levels were higher among organizations exhibiting higher virtuousness scores.

These studies do not allow us to make causal assumptions about the link between virtuousness and performance or profitability, but more recent longitudinal studies by these researchers do establish a more causal link.[120] Additional research by McKinsey & Company found higher levels of social cohesion and inclusion generated feelings of fairness, involvement, respect, and equality, which were subsequently predictive of work effectiveness, employee engagement, and employee well-being.[121]

Though more research needs to be done to test interventions directed at increasing social connection and belonging at work, especially in the emerging hybrid work environment, there is enough research to support an investment in a culture of connection and belonging. So, what can workplaces do to address this second element of workplace spirituality? The next section provides many suggestions for addressing structural, functional, and quality connections within the emerging hybrid workplace.

Application to Practice

Dr. Holt-Lunstad's three elements of social connection is a practical framework for fostering a culture of connection and belonging.[122] Structural social connection can be fostered by implementing strategies that increase the likelihood that people will have the opportunity to interact meaningfully with one another as part of their working lives. For employees who report to a common working location, the configuration of the workplace can influence how frequently employees can connect. For example, open office spaces with central, accessible, inviting, and comfortable gathering places (e.g., break areas, recreation areas, informal meeting spaces) can encourage employees to meet face-to-face rather than text, email, or phone one another. Access to quiet, private spaces for one-on-one or small-group conversations is important as well.

Virtual work arrangements can make provision of structural support a challenge, but with some creativity, it is not insurmountable. Digital spaces can be created that allow employees to drop into casual conversations with others, and virtual experiential events can be created with all levels of leadership encouraging participation. When the global pandemic required employees to work from home indefinitely, global consulting organization Deloitte created virtual teleconference happy hour events that focused on building relationships and social connections. Teams and work groups got creative and started experimenting with new ways to have fun "together" in a virtual way, such as taking a virtual tour of an animal sanctuary together or incorporating moments of fun into the start of virtual meetings. The focus was on personal connections rather than on transactional work interactions.[123]

Companies can address functional support by improving the depth of interactions that occur between co-workers. If the only opportunity for connection between employees is a task-oriented meeting, employees can feel they are only valued for the work that they do and may not perceive co-workers care about their feelings or are available to support them in ways not directly related to a shared work project. This was something I struggled with earlier in my career. I went into every work interaction with an agenda, objectives, and focus on meeting the purpose of the meeting. When I started paying more attention to the quality of my work relationships on my path from burnout to thriving, one of my strategies was being more intentional about sharing elements of my personal life with others and inviting my direct reports to do the same with me. I started to ask more genuine questions that invited people to bring more of themselves into the conversation. When I did so, I noticed that meetings seemed less tedious and depleting, which left me feeling more energized as I transitioned back to work. As I got better at weaving elements of personal connection into my work conversations, other people noticed. On one collaborative research project, I received many positive comments from people about how much they enjoyed our phone conversations and my ability to build relationships while also accomplishing project needs on the call.

Jobs where interaction with co-workers is primarily transactional make building deeper relationships a challenge. A strategy for increasing functional support is to first create "space" within the process of how work gets done to encourage employees to talk about topics other than the immediate work at hand. This can be as simple as starting every meeting with ten minutes of sharing about what's going on in one another's lives. Managers and supervisors can be intentional about using appreciative inquiry techniques to invite employees to share stories about their lives outside of work or to recognize team members for helping them feel supported. Such interactions should be grounded in vulnerability and authenticity, which leaders can first role model. The CEO at my previous job incorporated this strategy with our largely virtual team. Our weekly team huddles would start with a round robin sharing time that might be as simple as checking in on how we were feeling or asking us what gave us the most joy over the weekend. One day, we were all tasked with finding our favorite healthy cooking gadget for an impromptu "show and tell." In some meetings, this sharing time ran a bit long, especially if sharing surfaced a significant challenge a team member was struggling with. The CEO would adjust the agenda to ensure the highest priority business needs were met and push the remaining items into the next week's agenda or find alternative ways to get asynchronous feedback from the team. Holding space to honor and be sensitive to one another's challenges was prioritized above addressing non-essential business that could be pushed out until the next meeting. Though many team leaders may not have strong appreciative inquiry or authentic relating skills, these are teachable skill sets that everyone can master with intentional practice.

The third component of social connection, quality support, is fostered when social connections increase trust, inclusion, collaboration, and a spirit of positivity. Brandon Peele summarizes some of the research around effective development of social support within teams in his book *Purpose Work Nation*.[124] Group interactions must be designed to support psychological safety, allowing sharing of uncomfortable feelings, or designed to admit mistakes. Care should also be taken to nurture authentic connections. This is more likely to occur in smaller groups of people (six or fewer) and when groups are composed of peers at the same level of leadership or responsibility within the organization. For remote workers, digital technology has enabled small-group work with virtual breakout rooms. A larger group meeting may begin with all participants sharing and receiving the same information, but smaller breakout groups can be incorporated to discuss business applications, to brainstorm, or to identify solutions. The groups can be reconvened into the large-group setting to report out themes or insights. According to Peele, this is more likely to occur when small groups are formed with attention to diversity in terms of gender, race, and ethnicity. Optimizing diversity in terms of age can also be helpful if power dynamics are not an issue because older employees will more likely hold leadership positions than younger employees. Optimizing diversity for age should be sensitive to hierarchical relationships.

It is helpful to have leaders at all levels, including informal team leaders, role model these types of interactions. Leadership training is one way to ensure all leaders understand the importance of addressing high-quality social connectedness for individual, team, and organizational performance. Workplace well-being initiatives can incorporate education, skills training, and opportunities to practice positive social connectedness, all of which contribute to a greater sense of spiritual well-being in the workplace. Organizational values statements, written policies, and performance metrics can also prioritize the importance of how co-workers treat one another so relational dynamics are held at the same level of importance as what individuals and teams accomplish.

Employee experience data gathered in employee polls and surveys can help monitor the extent to which employees report having access to frequent social connection opportunities, perceiving interactions with co-workers are positive, and feeling there is a spirit of positivity, authenticity, vulnerability, inclusion, and trust in their social interactions at work. Organizations must set expectations for and enforce policies related to worker behaviors. Incivility, disrespect, rudeness, condescension, discrimination, and bullying should be discouraged and addressed. This requires policies, processes, mechanisms, and norms that allow employees to report mistreatment without fear of retribution. All workplaces are faced with challenges, deadlines, misunderstandings, and mistakes. It can be helpful for forgiveness to be valued and practiced. Forgiveness is the action of releasing negative thoughts, feelings, and behaviors toward someone who has hurt or offended another.[125] A growing body of research demonstrates a positive link among forgiveness of one's co-workers, higher levels of individual well-being, and more supportive relationships with co-workers.[126]

Much of the work of fostering a culture of connection and belonging can be embedded into the way work gets done within an organization. The emphasis is less about adding new elements to a well-being initiative (though relationship and communication skill building workshops and trainings can be helpful) and more about recognizing and encouraging behaviors and interactions that foster connection and belonging. The following actions require intention and attention: encouraging the use of enabling and affirming language, reminding employees to practice compassion and kindness toward one another, encouraging team members to reach out to one another for support and to accept support when it is offered, and helping teams overcome grievances and frustrations. This can be as simple as making it a point to remember and acknowledge important milestones, such as birthdays and service anniversaries, with a comment, with a handwritten note, or by picking up an extra coffee on the way into a meeting with them. Pause to ask about photos on desktops or computer screensavers. Get curious and find out what hobbies people like or what types of activities co-workers enjoy on the weekends. If you are a leader of a team or a supervisor, pay attention to personal priorities and goals that are mentioned by team members and make it a point to follow up and ask about them.

Creating a culture of connection and belonging starts with an individual, team, or organization identifying or naming the kinds of relational interactions and behaviors that foster connection and belonging. Invite co-workers into a conversation about what elements of connection building are comfortable for them, being sensitive that not all people feel comfortable sharing elements of their personal life with their co-workers. The next step is to observe or notice the difference between the intention and actual behaviors. Norms are created as individuals and teams increase the energy around naming and noticing the desirable ways of relating and discouraging the undesirable ways of relating. What gets measured and recognized by leaders tends to get the most attention, and that's where elevating relational behaviors as a key performance metric can help.

As I mentioned earlier, when it comes to fostering social connection and belonging at work, some may feel that these practices are "nice-to-haves" and non-essential to the real business of meeting goals and objectives. Therefore, workplaces must develop mechanisms to give *how* work gets done (in effect, how we treat one another at work and behave in our work tasks) equal weight and attention as completing tasks and deliverables. For example, key performance indicators (KPIs) and organizational scorecards or dashboards can include objective measures of how people perceive they are treated within their work interactions. Such employee perception measures should be given equal priority to measures of business performance.

Addressing cultural norms related to how we interact with one another at work is complicated. There are many different strategies that companies can use to influence interpersonal and team dynamics. As you will see in the employer examples that follow, shifting these norms may necessitate a tectonic shift in attitudes, values, and communications, as well as in policies and practices. This was the case for Softway, a case that summarizes how one organization successfully transformed its toxic workplace culture over the period of several years.

For other organizations where essential norms related to respect and caring exist, efforts might be more focused on fostering psychological safety or authentic relating behaviors. This was the case for Google when the company had to shift from an emphasis on face-to-face connections to virtual connections due to the pandemic. As they experimented with virtual connection opportunities, they intentionally incorporated authentic relating practices. Such practices aim to create a safe, intentional space that creates meaningful and enjoyable connections with others.[127] The movement toward more authentic relating was paved by Google's previous efforts to create a more psychologically safe workplace environment, one characterized by high levels of trust and mutual respect among team members and which helped team members feel more comfortable being themselves.

Employer Examples

Google

With more than 90,000 employees across the United States, Google is well recognized as an "employer of choice" due to its rich array of innovative employee benefits and perks as well as strong ratings on external workforce surveys. Like many organizations in the technology sector, Google is known for its workplace environment features with innovative sustainable architecture, embedded exposure to nature across its sprawling campus, provision of free or subsidized nutritious food choices, and a wide array of spaces that are conducive to employee collaboration. The onsite dry cleaning, fitness services, restaurants, fresh juice bars, and nap rooms make it convenient and tempting for employees to spend a majority of their waking hours at work.

When the pandemic forced employers to shift to remote working arrangements, most employees lost access to the onsite amenities and face-to-face collaborative working styles they were accustomed to. Many Silicon Valley organizations, including Google, were aware of national trends related to loneliness and isolation prior to the pandemic, and they designed their workplace environments to support more employee connections and collaboration at work. Though Google had programs and initiatives aimed at building community among Googlers prior to the pandemic, Google began working with thought leader Charles Vogl in 2019 to incorporate the seven principles for belonging, which he details in his book *The Art of Community*, into Google's culture of health and performance.[128] According to Vogl, genuine community includes a deeper sense of care and concern for one another, a sense of belonging, and a foundation for sustained friendship.

As the pandemic lingered and work-from-home mandates were extended, Vogl was asked to translate the principles for building community and belonging into a digitally mediated format. He encouraged Google to begin experimenting with an idea he called the Campfire Principle. The Campfire Principle teaches that workplace gatherings intended to connect participants must be hosted as small, intimate experiences with enough time for deep conversations and relationship building. The resulting program became known as "Community Campfires," which were initially launched within a collaborative network of national thought leaders working with Google to address human thriving.

The format of the weekly Community Campfires started with hour-long digital gatherings that relied on widely available interactive video conferencing technology. Initial gatherings established guidelines and boundaries for interaction that promoted authentic relating, psychological safety, and personal connection. Vogl facilitated the weekly groups, ensuring boundaries and norms were established to encourage vulnerability and personal storytelling. He also created a consistent structure for the gatherings. Each session opened with a review of guidelines to ensure confidentiality and promote a safe space for sharing. Once invited members were gathered, a one-minute period of silence was observed to ground attendees in the practice of bringing their attention to the present moment. It also helped punctuate the transition between "gathering time" (the time at the start of the meeting when people are logging onto the meeting platform and greeting one another) and "gathered time" (the remainder of the meeting when all who are expected to attend have arrived and are ready to engage). After the moment of silence, a discussion prompt was introduced, which encouraged individuals to set aside their professional personas and bring their fullest, most authentic selves into the discussion. This segued into thirty- to forty-five-minute digital breakout groups, which were comprised of three to four individuals and optimized to represent diverse perspectives. These groups were peer-moderated, meaning each member of the group held shared responsibility for facilitation of the discussion. After the breakout groups, members were invited to reconvene as a larger group and share themes (but not individually identified information) from their breakout groups.

Lisa Olson, former program manager with EXOS at Google, was an instrumental part of the initial Community Campfire experiment and remembers first-time participants referring to their experience as "magic" because people felt comfortable enough to bring the reality of their circumstances into the group. The Community Campfires were offered at a time when people felt most alone, scared, and isolated. They welcomed the opportunity to talk to others about what they were experiencing. Laughter and tears were shared among strangers in these Community Campfires and people were often surprised at how comfortable it felt to bring their authentic selves into these conversations. As a facilitator of some of the pilot Community Campfires, Lisa attributes this "magic" to the intentionality that went into the invitations, the opening welcoming remarks for each session, the careful review of guidelines that created a virtual container that felt welcoming, safe, caring, and trusting enough to encourage authenticity and vulnerability amongst participants.[129]

The Community Campfires were initially created as a short-term experiment but due to their popularity, they continued for more than a year. Community Campfire participants began to connect (primarily virtually) outside of the weekly gatherings, and word began to spread within Google about the impact they were having on creating richer connections and a community of caring. Several original participants extemporaneously used the description "family" to describe the relationships they developed within the experimental program. Surveys of initial Campfire participants indicated 100% of them felt the gatherings were a valuable use of their time. One person added, "This was truly one of the best experiences I have had while working from home during this pandemic! I've been having a hard time meeting new people where I live, and these campfire meetings helped improve my mental health a lot and gave me a sense of belonging."

Based on the success of the pilot, Google decided to train members of the initial experiment to lead several series of Community Campfires with a broader group of employees within Google. As Google shared in communications about the initial pilot experiment, "In testing thus far, Community Campfire experiments have led to the formation of mutual concern, shared goals and emerging activities for people to participate in together, as colleagues and genuine friends."

Employees were asked to commit to attending a six-week series of weekly gatherings, which were offered at many different days of the week and times of day to accommodate multiple time zones and work schedules. Employee response to the pilot series was positive, and more than 100 Google employees were eventually trained to facilitate Community Campfires within the broader organization.

Evaluation is ongoing, but initial participant response confirms the effectiveness of the format for enriching connections and promoting more authentic and personal conversations. Individual testimonials indicate how the relationships formed as part of these Community Campfires have become an enduring support for many members, with some reporting they were "a lifeline I clung to" through the pandemic. According to Google Health and Performance Innovation Partnerships Manager Michelle Railton, "Community Campfires have the potential to provide a safe, scalable format for people to feel heard, supported and connected to each other with technology as their medium and enabler (rather than an inhibitor). On a personal level, I've found them to be a transformational and moving experience to be part of. The time together helps me build stronger connections, uncover new knowledge from others' wisdom and quite unexpectedly, experience healing. I feel safe and supported to bring my most vulnerable and authentic self."[130]

Softway

Softway is a technology solutions company with a focus on building resilient, inclusive, and high-performing companies. The company was nearly bankrupt in 2015 when its CEO decided to make a dramatic 180-degree shift from a toxic workplace culture to one grounded in a more "loving" way of doing business. The company's remarkable journey from near bankruptcy to growth and profitability is documented in a book, *Love as a Business Strategy*, written by four members of Softway's leadership team.[131] It began when the company's founder, president, and CEO decided that he wanted to do things differently on the heels of a massive 33% reduction-in-force that was executed in a single hour on a Monday morning using what was considered by many organizations as "standard corporate layoff procedure." His executive leadership team designed the layoff protocols and communications and wouldn't allow him to be directly involved in the process. He expressed misgivings but was assured this was the right way to do things.

Being party to a ruthless, cruel, and dehumanizing process led to his process of deep soul-searching as he grappled with who he was as a leader. The soul searching led him to make a commitment to radically shift how his company would operate going forward to emphasize a more caring, compassionate approach. Within days of deciding to do so, he called an all-hands meeting of both office locations and shared his vision for a "culture of love" at Softway, inviting all employees to join him in creating a more caring and inclusive culture. He admitted at the time that he wasn't sure what a culture of love would look like other than it would be characterized as a deep-rooted, intrinsic care for one another.

It didn't happen overnight, but over time, Softway leaders identified the mindsets, behaviors, and attitudes that were essential to the people-first culture they were trying to create. Once the desired mindsets, behaviors, and attitudes were named by leadership and communicated to employees, it became everyone's job to notice when they were and weren't present and to hold one another accountable to living out the desired actions in day-to-day communications, interactions, and operations involved in running a company. Over a period of years, their culture shifted to one characterized by inclusion, trust, vulnerability, empathy, empowerment, and forgiveness.

Inspired by a visit to Southwest Airlines headquarters in Dallas, Softway's leadership team adopted a servant leadership framework: a set of practices in which leaders put the needs of their team before themselves. All employees committed to living out the new vision and goals to put people at the center of how work got done. With plenty of missteps and experimentation, they learned to practice humility, authenticity, gratitude, and the act of asking for and giving forgiveness. Many of the executive leaders calling the shots during layoffs left the organization when the CEO first announced the shift toward a more caring culture. This allowed hiring, onboarding, and talent retention practices to place emphasis on encouraging the new behaviors they wanted to normalize. Over time, more attention was paid to policies, processes, and technology tools to ensure they reflected a people-first strategy and a more caring culture.

Softway leaders attribute the business outcomes they observed in the years following their commitment to create a culture of love to a shift from a focus on profit margins to a focus on Softway's employees. By the end of the first year following the massive layoff, Softway went from not being able to make payroll to a return to profitability. Within three years, revenue tripled, all company debts were paid off, project sizes had increased by 750%, average account size had increased by 985%, client retention increased from 60 to 90%, and attrition rates fell from 30 to 12%. Employee testimonials talk about Softway colleagues as family members and note strong feelings of belonging and connection. Softway's journey led them to formalize their strategy into six pillars of high performance (inclusion, empathy, vulnerability, trust, empowerment, and forgiveness), which they not only advertise and celebrate as a market differentiator, but also share through free web-based resources, an ongoing podcast, and Seneca Leaders training.[132]

Softway doesn't pretend to have reached a state of utopian perfection where messy interactions don't happen and people never offend or hurt one another's feelings. Mistakes do happen because it comes with the territory of being human together. The key to its success is in how employees respond to such interactions. They name and notice how specific behaviors promote or diminish the culture they are striving for and make an effort to correct what needs to be corrected. People still choose to leave the company and sometimes work is a drag, but they strive to create a culture where the majority of the work experience is engaging, one's skills are put to good use, and people feel like the work they are doing matters. Those intentions seem to have gone a long way toward sustainable success for a company that couldn't make payroll six years ago.

These two employer examples showcase how building connection at work is accomplished through intentional efforts to name, notice, and normalize specific interpersonal and relationship behaviors. Establishing a culture of connection and belonging necessitates identification of the relational dynamics and behaviors that foster respect, psychological safety, trust, and caring. Organizational, team, and group policies, practices, and norms cultivate desired behaviors and discourage undesirable behaviors. As we'll see in the next chapter on the third element of workplace spirituality, fostering a culture of transcendence, we often experience our greatest moments of thriving or our deepest valleys of despair as part of our interactions with others.

CHAPTER 5

HIGHLIGHTS

- Employee interactions and relationships at work have a significant influence on mental, emotional, and social well-being.

- High levels of social connection are linked to higher employee satisfaction, lower rates of absenteeism, better job performance, and lower levels of burnout. Loneliness is linked to more negative employee perceptions about the workplace, lower creativity, and lower productivity levels for individuals and teams. Organizations with higher levels of perceived social connection and belonging are associated with better financial performance and profitability.

- Managerial/supervisory relationships with direct reports help set the tone for how connected and psychologically safe employees feel within their teams.

- Creating a culture of connection and belonging is highly related to purpose because many people name specific relationships as their highest priority in life. Having a strong sense of connection at work can help work to feel more meaningful to employees.

- Creating a culture of connection and belonging centers around moral character strengths, which reflect how we perceive and treat one another. Cultural norms and practices that build trust, authenticity, respect for others, and inclusivity are essential building blocks for creating a culture of connection and belonging.

- Creating higher levels of social connection at work requires attention to three components:

  1. Structural support, which focuses on the physical and behavioral presence of others

  2. Functional support, which focuses on perceptions about co-worker support of us

  3. Quality support, which focuses on the emotional aspects of our relationships

- Employers can foster a culture of connection and belonging by incorporating these practices:

  o Identify organizational and team values that foster social connection and belonging (e.g., trust, respect, forgiveness, kindness, inclusion, etc.). Incorporate these values into policies, practices, and expectations for individual, team, and corporate performance

  o Configure physical workplace settings to foster informal, casual conversations between employees (e.g., with centralized, inviting, comfortable gathering places) o   Create digital connection opportunities that emphasize peer-led, informal, personal conversations that are not work- or task-oriented

o   Incorporate small-group interactions into larger gatherings to encourage authenticity and personal storytelling

o   Provide training to employees, team leaders, and formal leaders at all levels to encourage skill building in the areas of psychological safety, authentic relating, appreciative inquiry, and emotional intelligence

o   Embed more personal times of sharing into regular meetings, which allow team members to develop deeper connections and relationships with one another

o   Teach and encourage leaders at all levels to role model authenticity, respect, compassion, and inclusion

o   Add employee perceptions about social connectedness and belonging to employee experience and engagement surveys

o   Incorporate measures of employee perceptions of organizational values and practices that foster connection and belonging into employee surveys

o   Add relationship building skills to professional development goals and plans

o   Incorporate forgiveness training into workplace well-being programs

o   Incorporate appreciation, recognition, and kindness into team and corporate initiatives

A Culture of Transcendence

"Transcendence of the world is to act and to interact
without any self-seeking."

— ECKHART TOLLE

Transcendence as a Team Sport

It's 8 a.m. on a Saturday morning as I climb into the tour van with my work team. We arrived in Portland the day before to begin preparations for our organization's annual conference. The seven of us represent the totality of our non-profit organization's staff and we're located across the United States. We work remotely most of the year but come together as a team for the full week it will take to prepare for, execute, and wrap up the conference. Though we gather weekly for video calls as a team, the occasion of being together in person is the highlight of the year and we've made special plans for a morning of team building prior to digging into the lion's share of the preparatory work leading up to Monday's opening sessions.

Though our official meal policy as an organization requires an emphasis on healthy food options, we're making an exception to sample one of

Portland's local delicacies: gourmet doughnuts, which will be offset by a morning of intermittent hiking. One of our colleagues lives in Portland, and she took charge of the selection on behalf of the team, carefully considering each person's preferences. None of the really good doughnut places offered gluten-free doughnuts, so a colleague surprises me with a special dessert-like, gluten-free granola bar, insisting it is one of her daughter's favorites. Her thoughtful gesture helps me feel included and cared for and I happily joined the others in our indulgent snack as the van makes its way toward our morning hiking location.

We've been talking about the waterfall hiking tour for weeks and even the drizzle of rain in the forecast doesn't dampen our spirits. We laugh, joke, and poke fun at one another as we catch up on interests and hobbies. After about forty-five minutes, we arrive at the parking lot for the first stop on the tour. We buddy up according to our abilities and preferences, and I am touched when one of the competitive athletes on the team pairs up with a team member who has been training for weeks so she can complete the hike without using her walking cane. A couple of the pairs jackrabbit ahead as others take a more deliberate pace, all agreeing to meet up in the gift shop for a group photo at a designated time, before getting back into the van for a series of stops at various waterfalls along the guided tour. The combination of social time spent deepening our personal relationships with one another and the beauty of the waterfalls work their magic, offering some respite from the days, weeks, and months of hard work spent preparing for the week-long conference.

The hours seemed to fly by and all too soon we are back at the hotel, where some of us continue to a late lunch as others head to hotel rooms for a much-needed nap before we resume our preparations. We know from past experience that all team members will be relied upon to bring the fullness of their energy, expertise, gifts, and capabilities to execute their assigned duties with the highest levels of quality, customer service, and professionalism in the days ahead. Each team member will feel challenged in ways that extend beyond the intensity of a grueling schedule that requires staff members to attend to duties well before breakfast service opens to conference attendees and well after evening dinner and networking events end. Staff assignments and responsibilities consider each person's preferences and strengths, with a balanced eye toward ensuring adequate periods of rest and recovery.

Still, all have their own moments of being stretched a bit beyond their comfort zone into leading opening remarks, greeting prestigious speakers, coordinating interns and volunteers, and so on. Due to our authentic times of sharing during weekly video staff meetings, team members are sensitive to how one another will be experiencing moments of challenge during the conference, and in some cases, staff assignments are intentional in providing backup support to one another. In addition, team members are voluntarily proactive in their efforts to encourage, offer support, or check in with one another. For example, I am normally an early riser and am assigned to stop in and check on breakfast setup each day, letting conference food and beverage staff know if any aspect of our healthy catering menu requires adjustments before the first conference attendees are able to access the breakfast area. Being a coffee aficionado myself, I decide to grab an extra coffee for my colleague, who is not typically an early riser but whose expertise requires her presence at the registration area prior to breakfast each day. As I drop off her coffee, I check to ensure she has her favorite breakfast selections set aside for a break once her registration duties allow for it. The days unfold one after another, and true to form, there are unexpected surprises, things that don't go quite as planned, and the team needs to be agile and creative in finding quick solutions.

The final day of the conference arrives, and the unrelenting pace of the past five days finally begins to wind down. Nearly everyone is physically, mentally, and emotionally exhausted. Jubilation at the arrival of the closing keynote quickly segues to a welling up of gratitude for one another's support and care and professionalism throughout the week. As the goodbyes from departing attendees echo down the hallway, members of our team gather for a final team hug. We assemble in a circle facing one another and form a huddle with arms around one another's waists or shoulders. We lean into the weight of one another, the structure of our tightly knit circle providing auxiliary support for tired legs and aching lower backs. We take turns expressing appreciation for one another's special moments of support or encouragement, echoing words that had been exchanged in written thank you notes that we'd shared with one another the night before at the team dinner.

It is a bittersweet moment of relief that several days of welcome rest and recovery are ahead but also of sadness that we won't be together in person as a full team for another twelve months. I close my eyes for a moment and bask in the feelings of love and affection for each team member, reflecting on earlier times in my career when I hadn't felt as grounded, connected, or appreciated. In that moment, I feel harmony, belonging, shared purpose, and the satisfaction of achieving something greater than the sum of each team member's contributions. It feels briefly like transcendence, which represents the third element of workplace spirituality.

Third Workplace Spirituality Element: Fostering a Culture of Transcendence

Transcendence is often associated with a spiritual or religious state, but its Latin origins help us understand its meaning more fully. Its prefix, "trans-," means "beyond," and its root, "scandare," means "to climb." Thus, transcendence means to go beyond ordinary limitations, to have reached the condition of moving beyond physical needs and realities. It is the act of rising above and beyond something to a superior state. It has also been described as a sense of connection to something larger than oneself. Abraham Maslow defined transcendence as ". . . the very highest and most inclusive or holistic level of human consciousness, behaving and relating, as ends rather than means, to oneself, to significant others, to human beings in general, to other species, to nature, and to the cosmos."[133] Viktor Frankl emphasized a construct of self-transcendence that focuses on serving others rather than on fulfilling one's own potential. Researchers link self-transcendence to an individual's search for new perspectives, meaning, and well-being and it allows us to overcome self-absorbed striving for self-esteem or ego concerns.[134]

Consider your life journey so far. Are there peak experiences that stand out in vivid technicolor in your memory? Times when you felt a fullness of being that seemed to expand beyond you and at the same time to knit you together with some element of creation? I'll never forget the first time I saw the aurora borealis (northern lights) shimmering in the summer sky as a friend and I lay on our backs, transfixed by the vibrant colors. Transcendent experiences are often brief moments of time but can be life altering, catalytic, and transformational. They are often perspective shifting moments, sparking new insights or a deeper understanding or appreciation of people or the world around us.

At this point, you may be thinking, "What in the world does transcendence have to do with the workplace and why should my organization devote scarce resources to fostering it? Isn't this type of stuff best left to individual pursuits outside of the workplace?" Though the word "transcendence" might seem mystical and ethereal, rest assured the concept is measurable and the experience of it has implications for individual and organizational thriving. Organizations can do many things to foster self-transcendent experiences in the workplace. Future sections of this chapter will establish the links between this element of workplace spirituality, individual well-being, and business outcomes. And I would argue at the outset that when workers are able to experience moments of self-transcendence in their work, it creates meaning and connection as well as increases their desire to keep coming back to work! But before we begin a deeper discussion about the benefits of transcendence, it's helpful to better understand the concept, what factors foster transcendent experiences, and what emerges from them.

Experiencing transcendence can induce individuals to focus less on themselves and feel as if they are part of a greater whole with increased connectedness with others. Connectedness to one's innermost self, to others, to nature, to a greater life force are all elements of transcendence and it is often the awareness or experience of transcendence that people most readily equate with spirituality.[135] In this way, we can see how the three aspects of workplace spirituality (purpose, connection and belonging, and transcendence) are intertwined and mutually reinforcing. This aspect of spirituality plays a role in people's ability to practice more consciousness in their personal and work lives. Increased consciousness, the state of being awake and aware of one's surroundings and context, allows one to shift from relating to circumstances in life as happening *to me* to happening *by me* to happening *through me* to happening *as me*. These profound shifts in consciousness influence our ability to perceive, identify, relate to, and act toward ourselves, others, and the world.[136] They are especially important for anyone serving in a leadership role (in life or in work) because the ability to shift toward a more conscious way of leading is less reactive and more open, curious, and committed to a growth mindset. This ability to shift into a more heightened state of consciousness is fundamental to fostering well-being and can be embodied by individuals, teams, and organizations. Creating a more transcendent workplace can foster more conscious ways of living and leading.[137]

Yaden and colleagues[138] propose that self-transcendent experiences are temporary states that exist along a spectrum of intensity ranging from losing oneself in their work (often referred to as "flow" experiences) to the more intense and potentially transformative state involving the dissolution of boundaries between oneself and others. Physical manifestations may include a range of positive or negative sensations including warmth, lightness, vibration, shaking, hyperventilating, nausea, and vomiting. Perceptions of egolessness, timelessness, and a shift away from self-boundaries may occur.

Significant research has been done to help define and measure transcendence and to identify the circumstances or influences that might serve as precursors to transcendent experiences. Understanding these precursors is important because they hold the key to guiding organizations in how to foster a culture of transcendence. In other words, research helps us understand what conditions contribute to the emergence of self-transcendent states, which allows workplaces to incorporate those conditions into the workplace experience, enabling employees to more easily access these states.

Transcendence can be experienced by individuals regardless of their affiliation with a religious or faith tradition.[139] For example, many people experience awe, one of many transcendent mental states, in response to nature. One researcher's application of Viktor Frankl's work on self-transcendence suggests three kinds of self-transcendence, and he offers both theistic and non-theistic definitions.[140] The first kind of self-transcendence is associated with seeking ultimate meaning in life, which may include a connection to the divine or to ideals, such as goodness, truth, and beauty. The second kind of self-transcendence is associated with seeking situational meaning, which may include connection with spiritual values or being mindful of the present moment with an attitude of openness, curiosity, and compassion. The third kind is seeking one's calling, which may mean striving to pursue a higher purpose for the greater good in society or a life goal of contributing something of value to others. Though transcendence represents the third element of spirituality, it overlaps with the elements of purpose and connection. A single experience could represent all three elements.

Cultural differences probably exist in terms of the circumstances that contribute to feelings of transcendence. These include exposure to nature, to a work of art, to music or to a complex new idea; witnessing the miracle of new life or the passing of a loved one or a brief look into a stranger's eyes; and social events such as concerts or raves, especially when they are associated with rituals where synchronous movements are practiced.[141]

For some, prayer can also be a gateway to transcendence even for people who are not practicing it as an expression of a religious belief. Casper Ter Kuile, founder of Sacred Design Lab, describes the practice of prayer as ". . . being conscious—telling the truth—we really feel and think, taking what has been unconscious and bringing it into open awareness." He describes several different types of prayer that include expressing adoration or reverence, expressing contrition (awareness of how we've fallen short), expressing thanks or gratitude, and expressing supplication (directing compassion toward others).[142] Prayer can be practiced alone or in the company of others; in a sacred space or in everyday mundane spaces; inaudibly (in silence) or audibly (through verbalizations, song, or chanting); and using a variety of postures (sitting, kneeling, standing, lying prostrate, or dancing).[143]

The experience of transcendence is made more likely and experienced more fully when there is attention (presence), intention (directed toward something), and awareness (perception of the world around us). Frankl suggests it is important to pay attention to our internal and external circumstances from one moment to the next and to approach our immediate circumstances with open self-detachment and curiosity.[144] Contemplative or introspective practices, such as journaling, yoga, and meditation, help us to be more attentive, intentional, and aware of our inner and outer world. They also help us to practice self-distancing or self-detachment, gaining a broader perspective of our current circumstances, which helps foster consciousness and transcendence. We may not experience transcendence while using contemplative practices (though veteran, skilled practitioners may experience it), but with regular practice, they create the conditions that foster experiences of transcendence.

There has been a growing body of research on the experience of awe, which is one positive mental state associated with transcendence. In a seminal 2003 paper, psychologists Dacher Keltner and Jonathan Haidt describe awe as an experience that so challenges one's conception of the world it requires a conceptual shift or expanded thinking to make sense out of it. They also describe five different types of awe experiences, including threat-based awe, which has an element of fear or reverence. Stimuli, such as exposure to a powerful and charismatic world leader or to an extreme weather event, can evoke threat-based awe. Beauty-based awe is associated with aesthetic pleasure, with nature and artwork being common stimuli. Ability-based awe may be based on admiration of someone's ability, talent, or skill, as is the case with exposure to exceptional sports performance or artistic ability. Who hasn't experienced that wave of awe when watching athletes compete in the Olympic Games? Virtue-based awe occurs when one is exposed to a display of exceptional virtue or character, which might occur when listening to an inspiring speech or reading about the life of someone remarkably virtuous. I often experience this when watching documentaries about inspiring people or epic films. A final type of awe is based on an experience of a supernatural basis, as might occur if people thought they saw a ghost, an angel, or a floating object.[145] Wonder is a related state, described as a ". . . response to something incomprehensible, incredible, but not frightening."[146]

Self-transcendent experiences emerge in their own mysterious ways, and only recently have neuroscience researchers been able to reproduce some limited types of self-transcendent experiences in a lab.[147] Self-transcendent experiences are associated with positive emotions such as awe, compassion, wonder, admiration, flow, inspiration, peak experiences, love, and gratitude.[148] The role of the workplace is around creating the conditions and supports that foster these magical moments of joy as part of our work. These moments may be fleeting, but they can elevate our emotions and mood states as well as transform our ways of thinking about and approaching the world in a positive way. Much of the research on the positive effects of self-transcendent experiences is organized by the positive emotions associated with them, as you will see in the next sections on the well-being and business benefits of transcendence. Now that I've clarified what experiencing transcendence means and identified the factors that foster self-transcendent experiences, let's turn our attention to why it matters for our well-being and for workplace performance.

Link to Well-Being

As research on self-transcendent experiences is emerging, several studies link experiences of transcendence with physical and mental well-being benefits. Transcendent experiences allow people to rise above their own personal concerns and see things from a broader perspective, which may elicit positive emotions such as joy and peace.[149] Self-transcendent positive emotions include gratitude, compassion, and elation, which contribute to one's well-being.[150] Short-term benefits also include decreased anxiety and increased energy, insight, and sociability.[151] The power of self-transcendence to contribute to well-being is particularly powerful among older individuals, individuals with cancer, and anyone dealing with a terminal illness.[152] A study of elderly nursing home patients found higher levels of self-transcendence directly predicted lower scores on a depression scale.[153]

One of the most comprehensive discussions about the benefits of self-transcendent experiences is organized by the specific mental states experienced including awe, mindfulness, flow, peak experiences, and mystical experiences. Yaden and colleagues' summary of the research on self-transcendent experiences is worthwhile reading for those interested in deepening their understanding.[154] They report that experiencing awe is linked to altruistic behaviors (e.g., acting with selfless concern for others) and well-being. Studies of awe have only begun to emerge in the past fifteen years, but there are physiologic pathways that link awe with improved well-being. For example, one study found a higher frequency of awe experiences over time was linked to decreased levels of a chemical in the body associated with chronic inflammation, which increases the risk of developing cardiovascular disease, diabetes, and depression.[155] Other studies link experiencing awe with more positive mood states, higher levels of life satisfaction, and decreased materialism.[156]

Mindfulness as a self-transcendent mental state has been associated with heightened positive states of calmness, peace, encouragement, and perceived support; and with lower or reduced negative states of anxiety, depression, loneliness, or isolation.[157] A 2019 randomized controlled trial found a six-week mindfulness training offered to employees at a digital marketing firm reduced work-related stress.[158] A 2009 research review reported mindfulness-based training resulted in decreased emotional exhaustion, reduced symptoms of burnout, and increased mood.[159] Immune system functioning has also been increasingly associated with mindfulness.[160] Drs. Elissa Epel and Elizabeth Blackburn have done substantial research to understand the biological underpinnings linking mindfulness meditation to better health and well-being, including longevity.[161] Their research focuses on telomere length and an enzyme called telomerase, which are linked to premature aging and chronic disease in response to adverse life events and chronic stress. Their research and that of others has documented how loving-kindness meditation (a practice derived from Buddhist traditions that focus on extending unselfish kindness and warmth toward all people) results in longer telomeres and increased production of enzymes that protect telomere length.[162] Other research on the physiological impacts of mindfulness meditation used magnetic resonance imaging to measure changes in the brain, finding more gray matter concentration in the areas of the brain associated with learning, memory, emotional regulation, and perspective taking.[163]

There is some debate about whether the practice of mindfulness is a spiritual practice. Some might argue that it is not spiritual because mindfulness is about focusing one's mind on the present moment and letting go of making judgments; it's about awareness. Still others argue the practice of mindfulness is a form of meditation and it can be a spiritual practice based on the focus of the meditation. For example, meditation on scripture or reciting sacred words can be a spiritual experience of mindfulness meditation. The practice of meditation (with a spiritual or a secular focus) can help the practitioner to be more mindful, aware, and grounded in the present moment. Many companies have implemented mindfulness programs to help employees focus their minds on the task at hand, manage stress, and recalibrate more quickly after disruptions.[164] It might also pave the way for a self-transcendent experience, which is an important aspect of workplace spirituality.

The state of flow is another self-transcendent mental state that has received significant attention in well-being research. It is considered self-transcendent because intense focus and absorption in an interesting or challenging task can result in a reduced sense of self. Its experience is linked to positive emotions and has surfaced in well-being research as a component of engagement. Emerging research suggests that when experienced with other people, flow may be associated with social connection, which has many ties to well-being.[165] Again, we see the overlap between the three dimensions of spirituality.

Peak experiences (transcendent moments of pure joy, ecstasy, or elation) and mystical experiences (a feeling of being in profound connection with the universe, a higher power, or heightened consciousness) are rarer occurrences but have also been studied and generally found to be associated with well-being, positive attitudes about life, positive mood, altruism, and life satisfaction, often for eighteen months or more after the self-transcendent experience.

In summary, experiencing transcendence at work elevates our working lives from mundane to magical. However fleeting transcendence moments may be, they stand out in our minds long after they occur. They increase our quality of life and can serve as milestone markers in our memories due to their powerful ability to transform how we view life, our place in the larger world, and our sense of connection to those around us. It might be easy to understand how transcendent experiences contribute to individual well-being but less understandable regarding how transcendence contributes to business outcomes. Read on to learn more about how businesses benefit when employees experience self-transcendence.

Link to Business Outcomes

There is probably more research on the business benefits of mindfulness than on any of the self-transcendent mental states discussed in this chapter, making it an obvious place to begin this discussion. Numerous studies show that mindfulness improves brain functioning, emotional regulation, and positive physiologic responses related to stress, which can influence work (job, task, and safety) performance, workplace relationships (communication, conflict management, empathy/compassion, leadership, teamwork) and related workplace behaviors.[166] Others report a link between mindfulness and reduced absence, increased leadership trust, and increased employee engagement.[167] Goleman and Davidson summarize the research linking mindfulness meditation with staying calm and open-minded, improved cognitive abilities that allow people to perform complex tasks and think outside the box, and improved focus and clear thinking. All of these benefits help employees to deal more effectively with unpredictable environments.[168] I've certainly experienced such benefits in my own work life. A daily mindful walk leaves me returning to the workplace feeling more grounded and less reactive, which contributes to higher quality interactions with co-workers and clients. I often experience my greatest insights or moments of creativity when I'm on a mindful walk, which has contributed to problem-solving or mental focus when I return to my home office. Much of the content of this book emerged following a mindful walk!

Research on contemplative practices that are focused on benefitting others, such as kindness and compassion meditation, have been linked to decreases in discrimination toward marginalized groups and can reduce implicit bias, which contributes to a culture of inclusion and complements diversity, equity, and inclusion (DEI) efforts.[169] So, meditation practices incorporated as part of workplace well-being initiatives can increase the likelihood of transcendence while also supporting DEI goals.

Many studies link the self-transcendent positive emotion of awe with higher levels of kindness, generosity, ethical decision making, and prosocial behavior, which can contribute to more positive relationships with co-workers.[170] Here we see again how fostering a culture of transcendence is related to the second spiritual well-being element of connectedness.

Emerging research shows that leaders at all levels in an organization are more effective problem solvers and decision makers when they have high levels of holistic well-being, which includes elements such as awe, appreciation, flow, wisdom, vision, purpose, etc. Be Well Lead Well® executive coaches along with researchers from the University of Colorado at Colorado Springs worked with more than 425 leaders to explore the relationship between holistic well-being and leadership effectiveness.[171] Leadership effectiveness was measured by assessing five paradoxes that most leaders must navigate to lead effectively; e.g., assigning work to people without favoritism while also considering individual strengths. Holistic well-being was assessed across six dimensions (Thriving, Fuel, Flow, Wonder, Wisdom, and Thriving Amplified) as defined by the Be Well Lead Well Pulse® well-being leadership assessment. Leaders who scored high on holistic well-being were 38% more likely to report the ability to navigate the five paradoxes effectively. Executive Director of Be Well Lead Well® Renee Moorefield describes the role of transcendence: "Leaders with high levels of well-being reported more physical and emotional energy to engage in handling paradoxes but the spirituality-related elements of well-being may have also allowed them to bring a more transcendent perspective to the situation."[172]

The business benefits of self-transcendence are especially salient in health care settings, where caregivers must attend to the suffering of their patients while also managing their own experience of suffering given the life and death circumstances they face in their work. A 2010 study of registered nurses found nurses with higher levels of self-transcendence were more engaged, dedicated, and absorbed in their work than nurses with lower levels of self-transcendence.[173]

Earlier sections of this chapter helped define transcendence and identify the precursors to transcendence, which is helpful for guiding employers on actions they might take to foster a culture of transcendence. The last two sections identified how acting to foster transcendence can benefit individual well-being and business outcomes. Keep reading for a more practical discussion about how workplaces can incorporate this element of workplace spirituality into their well-being initiatives. It might surprise you how tangible, feasible, and practical it is!

Application to Practice

Though the nature of self-transcendent experiences can seem highly personal and individualistic, an employer can do many things to foster such experiences within the workplace. This is not intended to be an exhaustive review of all the ways a workplace can foster a culture of transcendence, but I'll focus on the few areas where there seems to be the most robust research and alignment with workplace well-being practices.

Meditation practices associated with promoting mindfulness and other self-transcendent positive emotions is one of the most popular applications of the research on transcendence. Due to the link between mindfulness and work performance, more organizations are implementing mindfulness training (e.g., Bosch, Google, Aetna, General Mills, SAP, Target, Mayo Clinic, and the US Army).[174] A 2017 survey of US white-collar workers found one in six had participated in some form of mindfulness meditation practice in the past year.[175] Because participation in training is often necessary for organizations to yield the benefits associated with mindfulness, it behooves organizations to reduce barriers to participation. Organizational supports for meditation practices include allowing employees to participate in training or practice during paid work time, providing quiet spaces conducive to practicing meditation within the work environment, leaders encouraging mindfulness by participating in the trainings or practicing themselves, and incorporating mindfulness or meditation moments into the start of every business meeting.

Another way to support mindfulness and self-transcendent flow experiences is to incorporate workplace processes and guidelines that minimize distractions and multitasking. Perhaps you've experienced the deep satisfaction and elevated energy that comes when you can focus your attention and lose yourself in your work. This kind of uninterrupted work time can increase the likelihood of having a flow experience at work. Having a substantial uninterrupted stretch of time at work is increasingly rare, as some estimate we are interrupted at least once every eleven minutes while at work.[176] To give employees more opportunities to mentally ground themselves and re-energize in between meetings, some organizations have implemented meeting policies that naturally incorporate a transitional break by limiting meetings to twenty minutes, fifty minutes, or eighty minutes. Research shows that introducing short gaps in between meetings can also help address multitasking during meetings, which interferes with the ability to fully engage and connect with others during meetings. Other organizations establish operating practices that require all attendees at meetings to silence mobile devices and provide a designated notetaker, so the remaining attendees do not need to have their laptops open during the meeting and can focus on discussion. Specialized software can be installed on network computers that permit employees to minimize incoming email or text message alerts while focusing their attention on a specific task or project. There might also be policies that prohibit meetings for part of or one whole day of the work week to allow employees to catch up on work that requires longer periods of uninterrupted time. During these times, expectations about responsiveness to non-urgent email or text messages should be altered to foster the aim of undistracted work time. There is also a significant need for role modeling and communications to challenge the false belief that multitasking increases one's productivity.[177] Managers and supervisors have a critical role to play in such role modeling. One study found that when managers multitask during meetings, their direct reports are also more likely to do so.[178]

Setting expectations and creating conditions for more focused and mindful work also applies to break and rest periods, which should be interspersed throughout the day. Encourage employees to eat lunch away from their computers and to avoid multitasking while eating. Even a simple pause to breathe and check in with one's hunger levels before eating can make a difference in mental focus and mindful eating. Practicing presence and mental awareness while sitting quietly, stretching, or walking are other ways to incorporate mindful pauses into a hectic work schedule. This can be very difficult in our hyper-networked digital world, where a single pause in the day often has us reaching for our mobile devices to check emails, update our social media status, or check out news headlines. A 2014 study found 67% of men and 25% of women were more likely to press a button to administer a shock to themselves rather than sit quietly and think without distraction.[179] This is why some companies identify mindfulness champions or ambassadors who role model and encourage monotasking.

Experiencing nature is a common contributor to transcendent experiences, and many employers design and develop their workspaces to increase employee exposure to nature. This can include adding more windows and skylights to new building construction or remodels to increase the amount of natural light, incorporating live plants and trees into workspaces, creating outdoor gathering spaces that take special care to feature natural elements, and developing aesthetically pleasing walking paths outdoors. Some organizations that cannot easily add sunlight or live plants to workspaces located below ground level or in windowless buildings install light fixtures that emit more natural light, add life-like fake plants to work spaces, and paint nature-oriented murals on walls and in stairwells.

Organizations not located in spaces with much exposure to nature can also create virtual reality (VR) technology spaces where employees can use VR headsets to immerse themselves in a guided encounter with nature. Research studies on self-transcendent experiences have used VR headsets to successfully induce some types of self-transcendent states.[180] Employees who work remotely, particularly those in urban settings, might be provided with VR technology to expose them to extraordinary natural places. Organizations can encourage employees to take advantage of natural spaces by encouraging outdoor meetings or walking meetings in natural settings. Allowing meetings to occur using voice only allows remote employees to participate in walking meetings, and meeting facilitators can incorporate moments of sharing what employees are sensing in their natural environments. Alternatively, employees in all locations can be encouraged to take some time to be still in nature without interruption during paid work time. Even a few minutes spent seated outdoors in fresh air and sunlight can be transformative.

Workplace rituals are another way to foster a culture of transcendence. Collective experiences that incorporate music, synchronous movement, storytelling, and the creation or experience of art can support transcendence. Rituals can be used to recognize beginnings, endings, milestones, and celebrations. Dr. Judi Neal describes several types of rituals in her overview of workplace spirituality research including welcoming rituals, layoff rituals, and silence rituals.[181] Welcoming rituals can be incorporated into new employee onboarding as one might celebrate the retirement of a long-tenured employee or celebrate significant service anniversaries. Layoff rituals provide an opportunity to express grief and the shared experience of loss felt by employees who remain with the organization. With the growth of mindfulness practices, many companies are now implementing silence rituals to begin or end meetings or to acknowledge instances when vulnerability or profound sharing occur. Casper Ter Kuile suggests rituals be developed with clarity around intention (what is being invited into the moment), attention (grounding individuals in the present moment), and repetition (making space to regularly incorporate rituals into the fabric of work life).[182] The key is not to let formality or the presumption that rituals must come from leadership get in the way of smaller-scale practices.

Kursat Ozenc and Margaret Hagen provide seven steps to designing workplace rituals including the following:

1. Set your intention (what point you want to make or emotion you want it to embody)

2. Identify a trigger (specific time, people, place, occasion)

3. Brainstorm ideas (identify possible elements of the ritual)

4. Identify a symbolic prop or act (something that sets the ritual apart and adds meaning)

5. Create a narrative with a beginning, middle, and end to the ritual

6.   Deploy it (do a dress rehearsal and act it out first)

7.   Codify the ritual with enough detail that it can be replicated and incorporated into regular practice.[183]

As you will see in the first employer example in the section that follows, they rely heavily on the use of intentional shared rituals and practices that foster mindfulness as part of how work gets done.

Employer Examples

OCB Holding Company Inc.

OCB Holding Company Inc. is a privately held family of food processing companies based in Canada. Main trademarks include Cordon Bleu, Clark, Paris Pâte', and Esta. Established in 1933, the company of approximately 400 employees succeeded in transitioning stewardship of the company to the family's third generation in 2007, a milestone reached by fewer than 5% of family-owned companies in North America.[184]

The organization's approach to workplace spirituality is detailed in a 1,500+-page dissertation written by the organization's former chief executive officer, J.-Robert Ouimet, summarized in the subsequent publication of *The Golden Book*, and operationalized as an ongoing experiment called *Our Project*.[185] The focus of this work is to nurture the human spirit of employees while also promoting a competitive level of productivity and profitability through an established set of core values and management activities that are organized into two Integrated Systems of Management Activities (ISMAs): One is economic, and the other is human. The selection of executives, managers, and administrators are guided by demonstration of strong leadership, competitive working conditions, required level of technical and professional competence, placing the human factor first, authenticity and humility, and having a heart of flesh and not a heart of stone.[186]

Three scientific measurement tools and planning tools support the management of the organization as it seeks to harmonize the activities of the two ISMAs. Every two years, the organization administers a survey of organizational climate to identify areas of tension in the execution of the two ISMAs, seeking to address what is not working as intended and reinforce what is working well. A different biennial survey identifies which activities of the human ISMA are most appreciated and considers which ones should be modified, abandoned, or replaced. Two triennial strategic plans are updated annually to document how the activities and strategies of the ISMAs will be executed and refined over time.

Though the management approach and model of the two ISMAs is deeply rooted in the Christian faith of its founders, *Our Project* is executed with a total commitment to freedom and personal choice to take part or not take part in the ISMAs while being on paid work time, and any hint of proselytizing or coercion is avoided. A summary of some of the activities represented by the human ISMA is provided below. Many of the activities have a ritualistic format to them with a specific intent, trigger, action, and narrative. Many of the activities also directly or indirectly foster mindfulness and there is a focus on quality relationships at work.

Sample Human Integrated System of Management Activities in *Our Project*

- Rigorous employee recruitment process including a meal for four and final interview before hiring an employee
- Coaching and sponsorship of new personnel for a period of six months
- Training on *Our Project* values and principles
- Spiritual guidance
- Spiritual support group
- Designated space designed for reflective silence and relaxation
- Prize of the Heart annual employee recognition award
- Bi-annual testimonial meetings where invited guests share human, moral, or spiritual experiences that have guided them in their lives
- Annual two-day retreat
- Community service days for all staff twice a year
- Community all-staff meals during paid work time
- Moment of silence before and after meetings
- Company prayer at the end of each board of director and management committee meeting

In terms of outcomes, the organization's website boasts the following sustained advantages since the project's inception in 1933:

- A healthy and dynamic company, that has grown and developed on the human level as much as it has in profitability

- Competitive salary, general remuneration, and a social security plan superior to industry average

- A culture of belonging which fosters employee development beyond their career path

- Devoted employees with a turnover rate below industry levels

- A culture marked by creativity and joie de vivre among employees

- Employee involvement in care towards the environment

The Fetzer Institute

The Fetzer Institute[187] is a private foundation with sixty employees. Based in Kalamazoo, Michigan, Fetzer uses philanthropic resources to build the spiritual foundation for a loving world. It funds innovators and organizations that research spirituality, engage in individual and societal spiritual transformation, and build a spiritual infrastructure for the future. It also operates programs to build a spiritual connection between people.

To fully realize its mission to "build the spiritual foundation for a loving world," the organization aims to create a workplace environment that feels welcoming and inclusive for all employees by upholding its four core values of love, trust, authenticity, and inclusion. Fetzer's founder first articulated his vision for a deliberate culture of cohesive community bound together by a larger purpose in the 1980s and that idea evolved over time as a Community of Freedom. The intent was to create a community where all people can come to work and be their full, authentic selves. In 2013, Fetzer initiated weekly "Community of Freedom Gatherings," which convenes the entire staff of sixty employees for three hours to deliberately explore how to live out the organization's purpose in all they do. These gatherings include the sharing of spiritual practices, relationship building, trust building, exploration of spiritual identities, and discussion of Fetzer's program vision and strategy. Learning topics range from emotional intelligence to mindfulness to spiritual parenting.[188]

In 2016, the organization brought in external partners to guide them through a participatory process of assessing the successes, disappointments, and stumbling blocks associated with the Community of Freedom. The robust process included co-creation of guiding principles and goals for the assessment; historical document review; interviews with a majority of Fetzer staff; group sensemaking; summary of initial findings; group discussion of insights and ideas; revision of findings with recommendations; and organizational application.[189]

Key findings from the Community of Freedom assessment report that activities have done the following:

- Improved relationships and morale and the ability of staff to tackle difficult conversations

- Resulted in spiritual growth and a sense of connection to something larger

- Supported personal and community healing following a period of significant organizational upheaval at Fetzer

Several opportunities for continued growth were also identified including the need for more clarity around the meaning of the Community of Freedom concept, the purpose of weekly gatherings in relation to the rest of The Fetzer Institute's work, and the tension between values espoused at weekly gatherings and Fetzer organizational policies and practices.[190] Fetzer acknowledges that the Community of Freedom is still evolving and remains a work in progress. It continues to grapple with the challenges of respecting staff differences in spiritual approaches, ensuring a sense of shared ownership and responsibility among all staff members to foster a community of freedom, and translating the activities from the weekly gatherings into other aspects of organizational life.

The employer case examples above have several commonalities. First, both organizations were heavily influenced by their founder's strong sense of spirituality, but the founder did not seek to impose his specific religious beliefs on employees. Instead, spirituality served as a foundation for the organization's broader mission, values, and practices. Second, both organizations strongly uphold the principle of spiritual freedom, which stipulates that all spiritual practices are voluntary and must respect the diverse interests and worldviews of the employees. Discussions of spirituality are intended to spark discussions about how to operate the organization in a way that aligns with its mission and values. Both organizations can also be considered purpose-driven because they have a purpose that transcends organizational profitability. There is also an aspect of ritual evident in both organizations. OCB Holding Company Inc. infuses ritual into its ISMAs, and Fetzer implements weekly, three-hour Community of Freedom Gatherings. A final similarity between the organizations is the rationale for including spirituality into workplace operations: it's a people-centric approach that aims to help the organization achieve its broader purpose by creating a culture that provides employees with opportunities to enrich their spiritual well-being. The approach represents a culture of transcendence because the approach helps employees to connect within themselves, with one another, and with the broader world.

CHAPTER 6

HIGHLIGHTS

- Transcendence is about connecting to something larger than oneself including to humanity, nature, new ideas, or a greater life force. Transcendence is measurable and can be experienced by all, regardless of their affiliation or lack of affiliation with a religious or faith tradition.

- Workplaces foster a culture of transcendence by helping employees and leaders to live, lead, and work in a more conscious way. This allows them to be less reactive, more open and curious, and committed to a growth mindset.

- Research on the well-being and business benefits of transcendence is connected to the experience of self-transcendent mental states such as wonder, awe, flow, mindfulness, compassion, joy, inspiration, and gratitude. They help us approach the world in a more positive way and with a broader perspective.

- Self-transcendent mental states are linked to decreased anxiety and depression as well as increased energy, insight, and sociability. Well-being benefits include better physical, mental, and emotional well-being.

- Substantial research has accumulated on the business benefits of mindfulness, which is a self-transcendent mental state. Mindfulness has been linked to improved work performance, stronger workplace relationships, more ethical decision making, and more acceptance of diverse people or ideas. Elements of transcendence have also been linked to leadership effectiveness.

- Employers can do many practical things to foster transcendence at the workplace including the following:

  o Support mindfulness and other contemplative practices through training programs, quiet spaces to practice during the workday, and flexible policies that allow employees to take brief mental health breaks during the workday. Brief mindful moments can also be incorporated into meetings and role modeled by leaders.

  o Support monotasking and discourage multitasking to foster the conditions for the self-transcendent mental states of mindfulness and flow. Shortened meeting times, specialized software that minimizes disruptions, leadership role modeling of monotasking, and promoting the benefits of monotasking can diminish multitasking.

  o Increase exposure to nature in physical workspaces and support exposure to digital nature experiences through virtual reality. Flexible work arrangements allow employees in all environments to get outside for a brief break.

o   Incorporate workplace rituals that help employees
    to collectively celebrate successes, acknowledge
    milestones, hold space for disappointments or grief,
    welcome new beginnings, and honor endings.

o   Expose workers to storytelling, art, nature, music,
    and other creative pursuits that are a gateway for
    self-transcendent experiences; they can be incorporated
    into workspaces and workplace operations.
    Incorporating these elements into group and team
    experiences can be especially powerful.

Workplace Well-Being Across Four Levels of Influence

"A system is never the sum of its parts;
it's the product of their interaction."

— RUSSELL ACKOFF

Tale of Two Cultures

Can you remember a time in your career when you were most energized in your work? A time when you got out of bed in the morning excited to engage in your work and felt like work was a place where you were encouraged, supported, and respected, a place where you belonged? I've been blessed to have experienced this during two periods of my work life: one was with an organization where I reported to an office every day, and one was while working in an entirely remote, work-from-home arrangement. In between those peak work experiences, I journeyed through a dark valley where I struggled to find joy and meaning in my work and where every aspect of my well-being was challenged. As I compare and contrast the peak experiences with the dark valley experience, the clearest differences had to do with workplace culture, which included

149

organizational priorities, leadership styles, and workplace policies and norms.

The peak experiences occurred when I worked under supervisors who valued their own health and well-being but also appreciated the need to support it in those who reported to them. In both instances, executive leaders commonly took a break during the workday to catch a workout and I was often invited along when I was with the organization that required reporting to the office every day. Sometimes this meant roller-blading with the CEO, and other times it meant accompanying my boss and a peer to a spinning class at the local YMCA. Even when I wasn't joining my leaders in a shared workout, they made it clear that it was okay to flex my work hours to catch a late afternoon yoga class or to get out on my bike before the sun set. Support for well-being extended beyond physical activity. My leaders took an interest in my professional growth and gave me room to select projects that interested me and to turn down those that didn't. They pushed me to stretch myself outside of my comfort zone, and they provided feedback and encouragement along the way. Many times, they invited me to collaborate with them on projects that elevated my skills and helped me meet performance goals.

The work environment itself was often fun. I'll never forget the time my boss and I organized a double-blind dark chocolate tasting with a group of fellow chocolate lovers at work. We each brought our favorite dark chocolate bar and developed protocols to ensure the tasters could not identify the samples by their appearance during the tasting. We enlisted an unbiased judge to support us in executing the protocols and collating the results. We developed specific criteria and a weighted scoring system, which was operationalized into a spreadsheet. That was two decades ago, and I can still remember which chocolate bars made top ranking and how dismayed my boss was when his bar didn't win the contest.

Work meetings were fun because attending to the critical work at hand was balanced with catching up on one another's lives and shared interests. Work travel was more fun, too. We built time into travel plans to enjoy the cities we visited and build deeper relationships with colleagues and clients. It might mean arriving at a city a day early or tacking some time onto the end of a visit. This kind of relationship building was encouraged even if this added time occurred during the work week. It helped that I counted several genuine friendships among my workplace peers.

Worker well-being was prioritized in terms of offering some of the organization's developed programs to employees. One twelve-week educational campaign was called "Soul Journey." It allowed all involved to select their own journey (e.g., a focus on meaning/purpose, a focus on personal enrichment/growth, a focus on values/beliefs) based on their interests. All employees embarked on their chosen journey at the same time, and each week the wellness committee organized events open to all employees. One week featured an employee art show where employees were invited to display artwork or crafts outside of their cubicle. Some employees were skilled in their craft and sold their artwork to interested peers. The Soul Journey campaign was voluntary and employees who did not participate in the campaign were invited to participate in the art fair. Fifteen years later, when I was working in the remote work setting, each member of the team took turns leading the group in explorations of what it meant to experience gratitude, joy, or compassion in our work with one another and in our life journey.

The culture of the dark valley experience was markedly different. The organization was made up of fewer than 100 employees in a single building when I started working there, and over the course of the next ten or so years, the organization grew to more than 500 employees located across several states. Unfortunately, my closest friends were among some of the first to move on to other organizations after the first of what would be many major organizational restructurings. During my dark valley years, leadership made it clear that workouts were something you do on your personal time and not during the workday. Now that I've been able to incorporate daily mindful walks into my work schedule, I realize how beneficial the daily break could have been to my total well-being during the dark valley years. Even a brief reflective walk would have allowed me to return to work more physically and mentally energized, allowed me to recalibrate my mood after a tough meeting, or given me time to reflect on my values. On really challenging days, I often incorporate prayer or music into my walk, which uplifts my spirit and helps me to work through feelings of discouragement.

During my dark valley years, I worked in a building that had a beautiful fitness facility, but it was primarily used before or after work or over the lunch hour (for those lucky enough to get a midday break). I recall with vivid clarity the day my boss pulled me aside and told me that I needed to have a talk with my direct reports because every day they took a walk around the outside of the building with members of another team. The route required the group to walk past the CEO's office window, and the CEO had remarked these employees clearly didn't have enough to do.

Team meetings under the same boss were tense because relationships between members of his direct report group were strained. We were peers at the director's level or higher but there seemed to be a constant battle of competing priorities. Supposed team building time out of the office turned into griping sessions over drinks. There were pockets of comradery, but it moved underground and outside of the workplace. Where my peak work experiences included frequent celebrations of birthdays, pro-

fessional achievements, and quarterly "all-hands" community meals on work time, the dark valley culture observed maybe one or two employee functions a year and they were held in the evening after core work hours, which made it difficult for evening call center staff or parents to participate. In the dark valley years, I also lacked the frequent encouragement and mentorship that I received from my boss and executive leaders during the peak culture years.

What's so striking about these contrasts is that I had a peak experience and a dark valley experience within the same organization but at different points in time. I continued to work with many of the same people doing similar work, but executive leadership had changed through a series of mergers and acquisitions. New colleagues were added to teams, and organizational structures shifted without an attendant concern for preserving a culture of caring, fun, and well-being. What's so strange is that when I left that organization, the nature of my work was similar and I continued to work with many of the same people, albeit in a different role with a different organization. Under more caring leadership, I thrived doing very similar work.

Returning to a workplace that valued a culture of well-being allowed me to heal and recover from the dark valley of disengaged exhaustion. Within six months, I returned to a default state of high performance, optimism, and excitement about my work. I became more intentional about setting boundaries to protect my well-being, with ample encouragement from my boss to do so. I was delighted to find myself within a work team that placed a high value on quality workplace relationships, and we worked hard to establish them even though we worked remotely most of the time. When a team member had a major health challenge or was grieving the loss of a family member, the rest of the team rallied around them. We absorbed work responsibilities and coor-

dinated amongst ourselves to send a gift basket or some other tangible demonstration of support. As I developed deeper relationships with my co-workers, I was able to identify a couple of team members who shared a similar faith tradition. We'd often reach out to one another to share life challenges and prayer requests. My work colleagues began to feel more like family, knit together with mutual respect for one another's strengths and concern for one another.

Culture change can be a daunting undertaking for organizations of any size, and it is beyond the scope of this chapter to describe change management processes necessary to shift a corporate culture, which is why working with other professionals or experts is essential to create a more holistic culture of health and well-being. Organizational development and effectiveness professionals are well versed in organizational change processes. This is also why a multi-level approach is necessary because leaders at all levels of the organization from frontline supervisors to executive leaders have a role to play in addressing the three elements of workplace spirituality.

Why a Multi-Level Approach Is Necessary

When I and my research colleagues first investigated the role of workplace culture on the effectiveness of workplace well-being programs, we were often met with resistance around how to apply the findings to practice. As researchers, we worked hard to identify measurable, objective practices that any workplace could adopt to support and strengthen their programmatic efforts. This included specific leadership behaviors, policies, and corporate communications. Even though our studies clearly linked certain practices to more effective well-being initiatives, we got pushback from some clients when we recommended they implement the practices. The resistance sometimes emerged because the individuals our organization was working with to design and implement their well-being initiatives felt initiating organizational change was not in their sphere of influence. It was far easier to focus on individual programs. And this is likely why a 2017 survey of US workplaces found only 17% of them were addressing what *HealthyPeople 2010* identified as "a comprehensive approach" that includes addressing the social and physical work environment, integrating programs into an organization's structure, and linking health and well-being programs to other organizational efforts.[191] Terry argues that even organizations implementing numerous programmatic efforts cannot call their approach "comprehensive" if it does not address these other elements and should not expect to see population-level improvements in health and well-being or related outcomes.[192]

A Culture of Well-Being Addresses Four Levels of Influence

In 1986, the World Health Organization (WHO) and several Canadian agencies released a report called the *Ottawa Charter for Health Promotion*, which emphasized the need for health promotion initiatives to balance efforts focused on individual lifestyle change with an equal emphasis on the creation of supportive environments.[193] In the case of workplaces, the supportive environment includes influences that hinder or facilitate desired behaviors.

The socio-ecological model has been recommended to guide the design of comprehensive, multi-level workplace well-being initiatives because individual-level behavior change efforts are likely to be more effective when physical environments, social/relational norms, and policies support the desired health-promoting behaviors.[194] Sallis and colleagues identified four core principles for the use of ecological models based on their review of historical and contemporary approaches:

1. Multiple levels of factors influence health behaviors including intrapersonal (individual), interpersonal (relational), organizational, and societal

2. The four influences interact (work in concert) across levels

3. Multi-level interventions are likely to be most effective

4. Ecological models are most powerful when they are behavior-specific

This chapter identifies concrete examples for the application of the socio-ecological model to the promotion of the spiritual well-being of workers as part of a comprehensive, multi-level approach to workplace well-being. Each of the four levels is discussed, with a special discussion about the important role of leadership, which operates across all four levels of influence. This is not intended to be an exhaustive list of all the ways in which an organization might contribute to spiritual well-being across these levels but rather an initial set of ideas that might inspire organizations to expand or enrich their current well-being initiatives.

Addressing Spiritual Well-Being at the Individual Level

Individual-level influences address the knowledge, attitudes, beliefs, skills, and behaviors that support spiritual well-being. Individual-level interventions often include assessment, educational resources, skill development and training, and individual coaching. Incorporating assessment of spiritual well-being into initiatives can be helpful for educating employees about the elements of spiritual well-being, raising self-awareness about one's level of spiritual well-being, and identifying areas of strength and potential growth. When re-administered over time, assessment tools also identify baseline population needs and evaluate how intervention efforts may have contributed to changes in spiritual well-being. A detailed overview of spiritual well-being assessment tools is beyond the scope of this chapter, but the Spirit at Work Scale developed by Kinjerski and Skrypneck has been used in numerous research studies demonstrating substantial reliability and validity as well as sensitivity to change over time, making it useful for evaluating intervention effectiveness.[195] The eighteen-item survey measures four factors related to the following: finding meaning and fulfillment in one's work; experiencing moments of joy, energy, vitality, or transcendence at work; experiencing a connection to something larger than oneself; and experiencing connections and trust with others at work.

Research demonstrates that higher Spirit at Work Scale scores are related to lower levels of burnout and depression and with higher levels of vitality, job satisfaction, organizational commitment, organizational culture, gratitude, life satisfaction, and self-actualization.[196] Though including spiritual well-being measures into a broader assessment of individual health and well-being is desirable, the emerging available assessments typically address only one or two elements of spiritual well-being. For example, Harvard researchers released a comprehensive Well-Being Assessment in April of 2021, which measured six domains: emotional health, physical health, meaning and purpose, character strengths, social connectedness, and financial security.[197] Its inclusion of meaning and purpose, character strengths, and social connectedness is a meaningful extension of many health assessment surveys that primarily address physical, mental, and emotional health; however, it does not include any measures that assess one's experience of transcendence at work. The Harvard assessment tool has been subjected to robust reliability and validity testing, demonstrating negative associations (higher well-being being linked to lower negative effects) with depression, anxiety, negative affect, and stress and positive associations with general health. Given its recent emergence, the assessment tool has only been tested on samples of US working adults and needs to be tested with other nationalities and culturally different populations. Its sensitivity to change in response to interventions has yet to be tested, and the forty-item survey may be less desirable than the eighteen-item Spirit at Work Scale discussed earlier in this section.

Educational content and skill-building learning opportunities are a strongly recommended complement to assessment of spiritual well-being. A systematic review of worksite health promotion intervention approaches suggested that health and well-being assessments with individual feedback were most effective when augmented by health education interventions. Applying this guidance to spiritual well-being initiatives would suggest that any type of spiritual well-being assessment be followed up with educational and skill-building activities that aim to increase an individual's sense of purpose or meaning in life, relationship building and connection with co-workers, and activities that contribute to transcendence (e.g., mindfulness training).[198] The Soul Journey program implemented by one of my past employers is an example of an individual-focused education opportunity.

Those implementing workplace well-being initiatives are often expected to demonstrate the value of investing in new programs or implementing new policies, so considering how to measure the effectiveness of your efforts is important. When it comes to testing the effectiveness of individual-level spiritual well-being programs, the greatest amount of research is in mindfulness training for workers. The previous chapter notes a substantial amount of research demonstrating the effectiveness of mindfulness training. Systematic reviews have found mindfulness training of individuals to be associated with positive changes in psychological outcomes, such as stress, anxiety, distress, depression, burnout, well-being, job performance, compassion, and empathy.[199] Scientific support also exists for programmatic interventions focused on promoting gratitude, kindness, compassion, and forgiveness.[200]

A growing evidence base supports the effectiveness of health and well-being coaching at the workplace. Many theoretical frameworks have been incorporated into contemporary coaching practices including the use of positive psychology principles, self-determination theory, social cognitive theory, the trans-theoretical model of change, appreciative inquiry, motivational interviewing, adult development theory, and applications from neuroscience.[201] The inclusion of spiritual well-being in professional coaching is becoming more established and may include helping clients identify or strengthen their sense of purpose in life and their personal gifts and develop stronger relationships with others. Faith-based coaching programs support the application of an individual's faith or religious beliefs to one's health, relationship, or workplace goals. Coaching can also support the application of spirituality to ethical decision making, especially for leaders.[202] Some companies hire purpose coaches to support individual employees in developing a stronger sense of purpose, and existing well-being coaches could be trained to expand their skills to better address spiritual well-being. In my previous work, I've had access to plenty of coaches who could help me work on healthier eating habits but no support was related to developing a sense of purpose, working more intentionally on my relationships with others, or prioritizing experiences that would add awe, wonder, and joy to my personal or work life.

Well-being initiatives can also support the spiritual well-being of individuals by adding corporate chaplaincy programs. Corporate chaplains are paid by a company or staffing agency to serve the emotional and spiritual needs of workers, much in the same way an employee assistance professional (EAP) would. The difference is that EAPs are trained clinical counselors while chaplains are trained in pastoral care, sometimes in addition to clinical care.[203] Chaplains often complement EAP services, and research shows they are positively perceived by employees. One study of five organizations in the United States found that chaplains support and enhance a positive organizational culture, help bridge cultural divides, and enhance HR's efforts in religious diversity and accommodation.[204] A follow-up study interviewed employees in nine organizations about their perceptions and experiences with chaplains, finding employees perceived chaplains as a demonstration of management's care and concern for them as whole persons. The study found employees felt the chaplains addressed their practical and social needs, met psychotherapeutic needs, facilitated urgent care support when needed, and provided religious and pastoral care. Researchers suggest chaplains can increase perceived organizational support of employee well-being, enhancing employee well-being and their commitment to their organization.[205]

Addressing Spiritual Well-Being
at the Interpersonal Level

Interpersonal influences address the relational dynamics, communication patterns, perceived norms, and skills that support healthy interpersonal interactions and behaviors. Interpersonal-level interventions often include assessment, educational resources, skill development, and training that engages teams or groups of individuals. Leadership training, mentorship, and team coaching may also be included in interventions. Development and implementation of activities focused on team performance are typically led by professionals who are trained in the organizational learning and development field, but the most comprehensive and innovative workplace well-being initiatives are partnering with such professionals to integrate well-being into personnel training. For example, the University of Michigan partnered with leadership development professionals to create a four-hour training workshop for supervisors, which provides information and a toolkit for fostering a culture of health and well-being.[206]

Some organizations are intentional about incorporating spirituality into work with teams. Barry Heermann developed the Team Spirit Spiral model to support the integration of spiritual well-being into team capacity building activities. His model identifies six stages of development with nearly fifty tested learning activities. The six stages of development include the following: Initiating Strong Team Relationships; Visioning the Future; Claiming Goals and Roles; Celebrating Team Accomplishments; Letting Go of Frustrations,

Conflicts, and Disappointments; and Serving Customers and Teams.[207] The Team Spirit Spiral model relies on a spiral configuration to represent the nonlinear process of team development, acknowledging that teams can move up or down the stages in the model based on their circumstances. These activities incorporate rituals, storytelling, and exposure to nature and have been tested in Fortune 500 companies, major non-profit organizations, and organizations of all sizes.

Team coaching is another resource that can be provided to support team performance, but training is needed to ensure the coach is well-versed in the principles of group dynamics and understands how to coach the team as a collective.[208] Spiritual well-being concepts most applicable to team performance focus on developing authenticity, trust, deeper levels of connection, and a shared purpose and values that influence team interactions.

Fisher and Phillips describe the values, behaviors, processes, and barriers that influence the development of high-performing teams.[209] They name psychological safety, empathy, and trust as foundational drivers of team performance. Training and coaching can help teams work through conflicting points of view and develop a shared understanding of acceptable team behaviors or principles for working together. One of the teams profiled in their book, *Work Better Together*, collaborated to create "Ways of Working" principles to guide how the team interacts and conducts their work. "Everyday Equations" prioritize the principles and values to guide team decision making. Some of their equations include prioritizing people over processes and shared success over individual success.

Laszlo and Brown identify some specific team and organizational practices that foster spiritual well-being by increasing people's comfort with bringing their whole self to work, practicing authenticity, and sharing important truths about their lives. Three of the practices are briefly described here and detailed elsewhere:[210]

1. Story Café: This activity invites team members to share stories about a central theme or core value (e.g., a place that holds great meaning for them and why) in small groups of four members. The format includes beginning with a time of silence to allow participants to take notes about their own story related to the selected topic. With the remaining time allocated equally, all team members share their story as the others listen actively and nonjudgmentally, without interruption. The activity promotes respect for different perspectives and authentic appreciation for others.

2. MetaSkills Wheel: This activity encourages team members to shift their attitudes, perspectives, and feelings about a specific work situation. A wheel is referenced that guides the participants through consideration of various perspectives or contexts through which to view the issue at hand. Some of the perspectives include viewing the situation from places of deep commitment to relationships, with playfulness, with an open heart, with a feeling of collaboration, from a place of inquiry, with openness to all perspectives, and with a deep sense of respect. Room exists to add one other perspective of the team's choosing. Decisions are made after considering a wide range of perspectives.

3. Dialogue: This conversational activity aims to draw out multiple perspectives and dimensions (feelings, stories,

insights, possibilities) to create a mosaic of collective understanding. Substantial research supports the development of different dialogue techniques, and many leaders and facilitators have created their own forms.

The authors suggest beginning with a powerful question that draws the group in to do the following:

- Shifting from knowing to wondering
- Shifting from statements to questions
- Shifting from certainty to curiosity
- Speaking only from one's own experience
- Turning away from debate
- Listening for information, not confirmation
- Allowing for silence
- Listening generously
- Seeking and welcoming differences
- Speaking with a fresh voice
- Being fully present

A facilitator can begin by reviewing these guidelines and approaches, creating a welcoming context, setting a time limit for dialogue, and opening with the powerful question.

Addressing Spiritual Well-Being at the Organizational Level

Organizational-level influences address the workplace practices, policies, processes, structures, and reward systems that influence cultural norms and behaviors at all levels. Organizational-level interventions often include physical or structural changes to the workplace environment and changes to or additions of documented policies, practices, and procedures governing how work gets done.

Organizations are complex, dynamic human systems because they are comprised of complex, evolving human beings and collections of human beings. Influencing change in policies, practices, and typical behavior takes time, is often messy, and is rarely linear. It requires intentional, consistent, authentic, purposeful leaders acting at all levels of the organization. This will be discussed further in the section on the special role of leaders later in this chapter. Though challenging and iterative, there are numerous examples of organizational transformation, which is often catalyzed during times of great challenge or crisis. The global pandemic, racial injustice, climate change, and political divisiveness have created a perfect storm of challenge for all organizations. Leaders are looking for ways to re-invigorate and engage employees and inspire new growth, which offers a ripe opportunity to bring new ideas into consideration, like expanding well-being efforts to include workplace spirituality.

Robert Quinn and Anjan Thakor provide many examples of organizational transformations and a set of eight steps for creating a purpose-driven organization in their book, *The Economics of Higher Purpose*.[211] Many of the steps can be applied to workplace spirituality more generally even though the focus is on the first element of purpose. One of the cautions they repeat many times in the book is to avoid the temptation to outsource organizational change efforts. Though external consultants can support and facilitate culture change, leaders at all levels of the organization must be willing to do the hard work required to identify a vision of the organization at its best, to role model the behaviors that support the vision, be authentic and vulnerable in sharing their own journey, and be vigilant in reinforcing the application of the vision to decision making and operational practices. More information on how to do this is available in their book and will be discussed further in the leadership section of this chapter.

The Health Enhancement Research Organization (HERO) launched a study committee to define and identify elements of a healthy workplace culture.[212] Of the twenty-four elements, some of them are more applicable to this chapter's discussion about inter-personal influencers (e.g., norms, training and learning, relationship development, sense of community, peer support, pushback, positive outlook), societal influencers (e.g., external community connections and altruism) and leadership (e.g., executive leadership, organiza-tional leadership, modeling). The majority of the elements apply to the organization as an influencer of employee health and well-being. Weaving support of spiritual well-being into these elements might include the following specific practices, which serve as examples but not an exhaustive list:

- *Shared Vision and Mission* exists when people are inspired by the direction and purpose of the organization, feel other employees are working to achieve the same goals, can link their own contributions to group goals, and see a shared list of principles are guiding decision making and behavior. Spiritual well-being is supported when employees are able to connect their personal sense of purpose to the kind of work they do or the way they work within the organization.

- *Shared Values* are beliefs or principles that guide the decisions and behavior of an organization, including employees at all levels. An organization with a culture of health positions employee health and well-being on par with other organizational values (e.g., quality). Spiritual well-being is promoted when shared values emphasize a people-first approach to well-being (e.g., compassion, kindness, respect, and care for one another).

- *Organizational Communications* support spiritual well-being when they openly communicate about the importance of strong workplace connections, support employee meaning and purpose in their work, celebrate success stories and resources available to pursue spiritual well-being, and promote an environment of compassion, inclusion, and respect for differences.

- *Recruitment and Selection* includes hiring practices and internal promotions and placements. These practices support spiritual well-being when the organization attracts, hires, retains, and develops individuals who have a strong sense of purpose, conduct their work in a way that fosters deep social connections, and contribute to an environment that supports self-transcendence in one's work.

- *Metrics and Measurement* systems support spiritual well-being when they provide visible and timely feedback to individuals, teams, and leaders about the extent to which their behaviors at work contribute to or diminish a culture of purpose, connection, and transcendence.

- *Policies and Procedures* support spiritual well-being when they foster employee access to spiritual well-being activities and resources. This could include permitting participation during paid work time, permitting flexible work arrangements, and establishing meeting guidelines and work practices that encourage mindfulness, self-awareness, respect, and inclusion.

- *Organizational Built Environments* can support spiritual well-being by creating spaces that foster passion, delight, and awe through artwork and exposure to nature and by applying the principles of Feng Shui (an ancient Chinese practice that uses energy forces to harmonize individuals with their surrounding environment). Dedicated spaces that allow for self-reflection and connection to nature and that encourage relationship building and social connection also support spiritual well-being. Technology supports for employees based outside of the formal work environment may include inspirational screen savers, online meditation resources, applications such as meditation timers, software that encourages periods of undistracted mental focus, and permitting employees to access websites that support spiritual well-being practices.

- *Employee Involvement and Commitment* to spiritual well-being can be fostered by establishing employee resource groups or committees focused on activities that promote purpose, meaning, connection, and self-transcendence.

- *Rewards and Recognition* practices reinforce desirable behaviors through tangible rewards, recognition, and career advancement. Spiritual well-being can be acknowledged by creating a Spirit at Work award that honors the values, behaviors, and practices associated with spiritual well-being.

Addressing Spiritual Well-Being at the Societal Level

Though many workplace well-being initiatives do not address it, strong arguments can be made for the inclusion of the societal or community level of influence as part of a comprehensive, socio-ecological approach. Such models of workplace well-being recognize the linkages between the workplace setting and employees' other life settings, such as the home/family environment, the circumstances of the commute between work and home, access to health care services, and the level of resources available within the broader community.[213]

Much attention has been given to organizations with a mission that transcends the corporate bottom line. Pioneering companies, such as Ben & Jerry's, The Body Shop, and Natura, embedded a social mission into their core business purpose in the 1960s. In 1994, John Elkington introduced the concept of the triple bottom line with its balanced approach to investing in people, the planet, and profitability. In 2003, Chris Laszlo proposed the sustainable value framework, and in 2010, the first B Corps emerged. In that same year, Patricia Abergene's megatrends book mentions the concept of Conscious Capitalism, and a few years later John McKay (co-CEO of Whole Foods) and Raj Sisodia wrote a book about it.[214] This evolving movement has elevated care for the planet and employee well-being to equal importance with corporate profitability. Social entrepreneurialism and Conscious Capitalism positions business as a force for good, which is a step in the right direction for societal well-being. And yet, some suggest that the promise of the sustainability and Conscious Capitalism movements have struggled to reach their full potential because some organizations' motivation has been largely driven by the need for competitive advantage and market share rather than on the deep conviction that business profitability is achieved by investing in a flourishing, thriving workforce and striving to have a net positive impact on the planet.[215] In *The Heart of Business*, former Best Buy CEO Hubert Joly argues these are not mutually exclusive pursuits. His model posits that investment in people is the first priority on the path toward meeting stakeholder needs and achieving business profitability.[216] A 2019 statement by the Business Roundtable reflects this thinking. The initial statement was signed by 181 CEOs who committed to operating their companies by investing in customers, employees, and communities in order to generate profits and return profits to shareholders.[217] How this commitment will be translated into action remains to be seen, but many of the organizations have been recognized for their people-centric business practices, which include addressing at least one of the three elements of workplace spirituality featured in this book.

Laszlo and Brown suggest businesses will thrive and flourish when their missions and values shift to a service-oriented approach that seeks to contribute positively to a flourishing world.[218] They argue that where the sustainability movement has inspired organizations to do less harm, the flourishing enterprise aims to make a net positive impact on people and the planet. In 2013, the Harvard T.H. Chan School of Public Health launched Sustainability and Health Initiative for NetPositive Enterprise (SHINE), which focuses on the role of business to contribute to human flourishing and sustainability.[219] One of their key collaborators is Levi Strauss & Co, which has been working with SHINE to assess and address contributors to flourishing across its supply chain, seeking to improve working conditions for all employees that contribute in some way to the production of its products. SHINE also collaborates with the Human

Flourishing Program at Harvard's Institute for Quantitative Social Science, which takes a multi-disciplinary approach to understanding contributors to human flourishing including family, friendship, spirituality, the workplace, meaning and purpose, and character formation.[220] Together, these initiatives and their collaborators aim to understand the effects of work on human flourishing and the effects of human flourishing on work as well as identify interventions to provide and promote employment, and that enhance the work experience. They've developed and tested a flourishing measurement tool in collaboration with Levi Strauss & Co, Allegacy Credit Union, Owens Corning, Aetna, and several major airlines.[221]

Societal-level influences address the community practices, policies, processes, structures, and reward systems that influence organizational interactions and influences upon the broader world. Societal-level actions may include the following:

- Changes to an organization's mission/vision that recognizes its influence on community well-being

- Establishment of a foundation that directs the investment of organizational resources toward community well-being initiatives

- Policies that encourage employees to volunteer in their community

- Initiation or participation in collaborative employer-community partnerships aimed at promoting the well-being of workers as well as the broader community

- Establishment of metrics that are regularly evaluated and reported to communicate about the organization's influence on community well-being.

Most of these actions require those responsible for employee health and well-being to partner with other functions or leaders in the organization charged with corporate social responsibility or sustainability efforts. It may be necessary to help business leaders understand the connection between community well-being and employee well-being. The Health Enhancement Research Organization (HERO), with funding support from the Robert Wood Johnson Foundation, has been working in collaboration with employers and communities to articulate the business case for employer investments in community well-being. Through a series of research studies and case studies, the Healthy Workplaces, Healthy Communities initiative demonstrates that "businesses have the capacity to provide leadership, direct their philanthropy, advocate for effective policy, boost volunteerism, and promote health within their organizations."[222] According to a report published by the Bipartisan Policy Center and the de Beaumont Foundation, businesses benefit in improvements to broader community well-being through increased consumer and employee loyalty, attraction and retention of top workforce talent, a healthier workforce pool from which to draw new hires, potential reductions in direct health care costs and indirect productivity costs, and enhanced employee morale, job satisfaction, productivity, and engagement.[223]

As you consider the workplace health and well-being offerings in your workplace, how do you see these four levels of influence (individual, interpersonal, organizational, societal) at work? Does the organization rely primarily on individuals to pursue their well-being or does it provide support through the other levels? Is employee well-being part of the organization's culture, perceived as a strategic investment in a thriving workforce? Or is it a menu of options available to those who have the time and interest? Has the organization been recognized by others for its health and well-being efforts? Has it extended its influence to support community thriving in some way? What more do you think your organization could do to broaden its influence in support of health and well-being across the four levels of influence?

Businesses tend to follow the lead of other successful businesses, making it critical for organizations that are investing in workforce and community well-being to share what they are doing in the form of case studies, working frameworks and approaches, and publicly available resources. Organizations like Softway (featured in Chapter 5) and Holding OCB (featured in Chapter 6) are two examples of companies that freely share their approach and resources with other businesses. Their willingness to do so exemplifies a higher organizational purpose to advance a more people-centric approach to work.

Today's workers are increasingly seeking to work in organizations that contribute to the good of society. Organizations advance the spiritual well-being of their workforce by helping them to feel aligned to an organizational mission that transcends bottom line profitability and giving them opportunities to contribute to their community through company-sponsored volunteerism and corporate giving programs that match employee donations to charities the employee cares about. If you've ever participated in a company-sponsored group community service project, you've likely experienced the positive emotions associated with helping others. It may have activated your own sense of purpose, helped you to build stronger relationships with co-workers and community members, and contributed to a connection to something larger than yourself, which are all contributors to your spiritual well-being. It's a win for you as an employee, a win for your employer because you'll likely feel more positively engaged in your work and perceive the organization more positively, and a win for the community.

The Special Role of Leaders

This section encourages workplace well-being practitioners to collaborate with professionals in a leadership training and development role within their organization to effectively engage leaders at all levels to support holistic employee well-being efforts. This might require well-being practitioners to develop a business case to support the link among leader well-being, employee well-being, and business outcomes, which is why this book cites so many research articles to support the effectiveness of workplace spirituality.

Leaders within an organization have a special role to play in advancing spiritual well-being at all four levels of influence. At the individual level, business leaders must learn how to cultivate spiritual well-being for themselves before they can hope to inspire others. When it comes to purpose, experts working with purpose-driven organizations assert that business leaders must first identify their own personal purpose and share it with others before they can hope to activate purpose for others in the organization.[224] This is why many transformational stories about purpose-driven organizations start with executive leaders authentically sharing their personal purpose story and reflecting how it translates into more meaningful and engaging work for them. Moreover, they must consistently live out their purpose because executive business leaders have an outsized influence on the rest of the company. If employees observe that senior leaders are not living out their stated purpose or the organization's stated purpose, messages about the importance of purpose are viewed with cynicism. And this is where many organizations fail in their journey toward fostering a culture of purpose and meaning.[225]

Tsao and Laszlo assert business leaders are most effective when they keep and role model flexible working hours, incorporate moments of mindfulness or self-reflection into their daily schedule, have a service orientation toward others, bring a sense of personal care to their interactions with others, work to protect and restore the natural environment, practice kindness toward others, and act with self-compassion and compassion toward others.[226] Such practices contribute to a leader's capability to make more thoughtful decisions, remain resilient to challenges, and influence positive workplace outcomes. As Dr. Renee Moorefield reports from her research and work with leaders, ". . . when a leader connects with their spiritual resourcefulness, it may help them better buffer stress; be open to diverse people, ideas, and situations; lead with greater clarity, purpose and effectiveness; and create workplaces where people thrive."[227]

At the interpersonal level, formal and informal leaders at all levels have a substantial impact on the behaviors of others and a substantial influence on employee well-being. Leading by example means visibly investing in one's own well-being, which can influence other leaders' behavior and workplace norms, inspire positive well-being behaviors by others, and help others feel as if they have permission to invest in their well-being as well. Leaders can also positively influence the well-being of those who report directly to them in the following ways:

• Helping direct reports to identify their purpose and link it in some way to their work

- Communicating in ways that foster authenticity, respect, trust, and inclusion

- Encouraging employee participation in or access to well-being resources

- Supporting employees in achieving their well-being goals

- Recognizing and celebrating employees for their well-being achievements

- Following up with employees to show that the leader cares about them on a personal level.

Unfortunately, many well-being efforts only seek to engage executive leaders in supporting initiatives. They might be asked to address employees in corporate communications or to show up at a new program launch event. Although visible executive leadership support is critical to the success of any organizational well-being effort, it's essential that leaders at all levels understand the specific role they can play to support their team's well-being.

As I consider my own journey as a mid-level department leader, I regret the times when I failed to role model a prioritization of my own self-care because it might have given my direct reports the permission they needed to invest in their own well-being at work. One of my co-workers often chided me for spending most of my time seated in my chair as I took one meeting after another, with hardly a break for lunch. Didn't I know that "sitting is the new smoking?", he'd often warn and leave research articles on the health impacts of extended bouts of sitting on my desk chair. I reasoned to myself that I was training for half marathons before work and did long bike rides on weekends. I had a standing desk installed in my office and used it whenever I was not in a meeting. At that time, I didn't know how to set boundaries around my schedule and assert control over the number of meetings that jam-packed my calendar every day.

One of the comments that stings the most from the 360-degree feedback I received, when I did the Human Performance Institute[228] leadership training, was that I failed to walk the walk when it came to well-being. Though I encouraged my team members to use the company fitness center during the workday, I rarely did so. I also worked through lunch instead of building social connection by enjoying lunch with co-workers in the cafeteria. I rarely regret the decisions I've made in my professional career, but I often wish I could have done a better job of showing up as a more authentic leader for my team when it came to role modeling work-life balance and prioritizing my own well-being. It would have been easier to do that if I'd been exposed to leadership training earlier in my career that encouraged me to identify my personal purpose and values and to consider how to live them out in my leadership role. Though I was exposed to management training, it didn't include the principles of authentic leadership, conscious leadership, or servant leadership even though substantial training programs existed at the time. As I reflect back on my leadership and well-being journey, I wonder how I might have been a more effective leader if my organization had incorporated workplace spirituality elements into leadership development and employee well-being efforts.

Developing leaders to positively influence their own well-being and that of others requires ongoing training and support. Most culture change initiatives start at the top of the organization because executive leaders set expectations and strategic priorities, steward company reputation and shareholder value, and serve as role models to other leaders. For this reason, the Human Performance Institute provides intensive executive coaching retreats that focus on identifying an individual purpose or mission statement and character strengths that inform how they live and lead, which informs the development of a Personal Credo. They also identify the physical, mental, and emotional daily behaviors that fuel their energy to live and lead with purpose.[229]

Though some organizations invest heavily in the professional development of executive and senior leaders, a minority support managers and supervisors with resources or training that help them foster well-being for their direct reports or teams.[230] Manager and supervisor support is critical because many employees identify more strongly with the immediate culture they experience within the context of their team. Leaders at all levels can be supported in developing spiritual well-being for themselves and in learning how to translate that into more effective leadership of others through individual coaching, leadership team development, implementing culture change initiatives, and specific programs designed for leaders. This is where external consultants, trainers, and coaches can be helpful. Seminal research and theoretical work on spiritual leadership was conducted by Louis Fry.[231] The model incorporates vision, hope, faith, and love. "The purpose of spiritual leadership is to create vision and value congruence across the strategic, team, and individual levels and to foster higher levels of organizational commitment and productivity."[232]

As leaders are supported in developing their own well-being, individuals should not feel as though leaders are pushing their specific beliefs onto others. Even in faith-based organizations where senior leaders commit to supporting a specific set of spiritual beliefs or practices, there can be explicit guidelines about avoiding proselytization in any form. Instead, they choose to lead by example, letting their behaviors serve as a guide to others. A US-based non-profit organization called the Global Dharma Center provides free spirituality-based leadership training, with testimonials from executives at Motorola, Tom's of Maine, Medtronic, Kaiser Permanente, Hard Rock Café', and many others. They assert that ". . . when leaders embody spiritual qualities, such as truth, righteousness, peace, love, and non-violence, those whom they lead are drawn to emulate them. They want to draw from the deep well of the leaders' wisdom and put that example into practice in their own lives."[233]

As decision makers, leaders can also influence or support organizational strategies, metrics, policies, and procedures that can contribute to well-being. This includes allocating budget for activities that support spiritual well-being and participating in them. Leadership involvement in community well-being initiatives extend this influence to the societal level.

Given the growing recognition of the strategic importance of worker health and well-being to a company's success, more organizations are starting to create executive-level leadership roles whose primary goal is to support company culture and the well-being of the workforce. This might include the titles of Chief Human Resources Officer, Chief People Officer, Chief Wellness Officer, or Chief Purpose Officer. Brower and colleagues suggest that by incorporating Chief Wellness Officers into the executive leadership team, health care organizations were better equipped to identify and address health care worker needs during the COVID-19 pandemic.[234] Others suggest that adding such a role can address not only worker well-being but also contribute to better customer experience, health outcomes, employee retention and business profitability.[235] The newest C-suite job title is the Chief Purpose Officer, who ensures work has meaning and that people understand the meaning behind the work; this includes educating and guiding employees at all levels to conduct their work in alignment with the mission, vision, and values of the organization.

Integrating the Four Levels of Influence

For many workplace well-being practitioners, developing an initiative that operates at all four levels (individual, interpersonal, organizational, and societal) is daunting. It's even more challenging when one considers all the different practices, policies, and programs that might be developed to foster a culture of purpose, connection, and transcendence. Achieving optimal outcomes for workplace well-being requires a comprehensive approach that addresses and supports well-being across several levels, but organizations willing to take the long view and invest slowly over time may decide to start small and grow their initiative over time. This is especially important if an organization's current well-being approach is operating at only one level (likely the individual level only) or has no elements that address the spiritual well-being of workers. For example, many organizations have started with mindfulness programs for individuals and gradually woven support for mindfulness practices through the fabric of the organization by doing the following:

- Communicating how mindfulness supports more purposeful living and higher-quality work interactions

- Incorporating silent spaces to practice

- Adding mindful moments to the start of meetings

- Developing mindfulness training specifically for leaders

- Allowing mindfulness mobile applications or timers to be installed on work computers

- Creating policies that allow workers to temporarily silence notifications to support mental focus in their work

Other organizations may start with the element of purpose and seek to incorporate it at multiple levels, as demonstrated in the ProMedica case study in Chapter 4. The next section offers guidance on how to develop a strategic and thoughtful approach to the design, implementation, and evaluation of workplace well-being initiatives.

An Approach for Small Employers

If you are working with an organization with fewer than 100 employees, you may be thinking to yourself that most of these ideas are only relevant to large employers with a big budget for employee well-being. When it comes to purchasing programs and hiring experts to support you, it can cost a lot. But fostering spiritual well-being doesn't have to require an investment in external programs or expertise. Modifying an existing organizational mission or vision statement that puts a priority on employee well-being as the driver of organizational success costs nothing. Working with employees to co-create a set of core values that takes a more people-centric approach to how work gets done does not have to incur a substantial budget. Instead, it requires working with individuals within the organization who can organize a series of employee interactive sessions that engage them in discussions about how to make the workplace feel more purposeful and work more meaningful, what behaviors foster connection and belonging, and what helps them feel like a valued contributor to something greater than their individual role.

Holding one another accountable to live out the co-created core values requires more courage than financial cost. Expressing an interest in and making space for employees to live out their individual purpose in their work takes creativity but costs nothing. Building intention to support workplace social connection and belonging into organizational policies and practices takes effort but not a large expense. And partnering with local community groups (such as the local YMCA, Habitat for Humanity chapter, or food bank) to bring your employees opportunities to contribute meaningfully to something bigger than themselves may cost no more than a half day of paid time once a quarter when all employees participate in a community service project or a charity of their choice. A great deal can be accomplished by bringing employees together to talk about these concepts and identifying ways to bring them to life in your organization.

This section of the book provided specific evidence-based strategies and tactics that organizations can implement to address workplace spirituality. This chapter exemplified ways to ensure you are taking a comprehensive approach by incorporating the practices into four levels of influence as well as engaging leaders across all levels of the organization. What's missing is an operational framework that organizes these ideas into an actionable, measurable strategy. The next section aims to provide additional guidance on how to create a plan that will serve as a blueprint for designing, developing, implementing, and evaluating your efforts.

CHAPTER 7

HIGHLIGHTS

- All workplace well-being efforts are more effective when they incorporate a multi-level approach that addresses four levels of influence including individual, interpersonal, organizational, and societal. Leaders have a role to play in supporting well-being initiatives because they operate across all four levels of influence. Most employers are not taking a multi-level, comprehensive approach to workplace well-being.

- Individual-level approaches to spiritual well-being address employee knowledge, attitudes, beliefs, skills, and behaviors. Individual-level interventions include providing assessments, educational resources, skill development and training, and individual coaching in the areas of purpose, social connection and belonging, and connection to something greater than themselves (transcendence). Corporate chaplaincy programs can be offered to complement employee assistance resources, and they are often well-received by employees who wouldn't otherwise seek employee assistance services.

- Interpersonal-level approaches to spiritual well-being address relational dynamics, communication patterns, perceived norms, and skills that support healthy interpersonal interactions and behaviors. Interpersonal-level interventions may include group/ team assessments, team trainings or workshops, team skill development, team or group coaching, mentorship programs, and leadership training.

- Organizational-level approaches to spiritual well-being address workplace policies, practices, processes, structures, and reward systems that influence cultural norms and behaviors. Organizational-level interventions include physical or structural changes to the workplace environment as well as changes to documented policies, practices, and procedures governing how work gets done. Other supports to spiritual well-being are creating a shared mission or vision that goes beyond corporate profitability to benefit society; articulating shared values that support more purposeful work and stronger workplace relationships; changing hiring practices to select workers who embody the values and behaviors conducive to whole-person well-being; and establishing employee-led groups focused on activities that promote purpose, meaning, connection, and transcendence.

- Societal-level spiritual well-being approaches leverage organizational resources and influence to benefit the broader community or world. Translating a broader organizational mission statement about making the world a better place into meaningful action is a necessary next step for many organizations. Potential actions may include establishing a foundation to invest organizational resources into community well-being initiatives, creating policies that encourage and support employee volunteerism in the community, participating in employer-community partnerships, and establishing metrics that evaluate the organization's influence on community well-being.

- Leaders operate at all four levels of influence. At the individual level, leaders at all levels in the organization must learn how to cultivate spiritual well-being for themselves. Spiritual well-being offerings related to purpose, social connection, and transcendence could be created specifically for leaders to help them understand the importance of their own well-being on leadership effectiveness and learn how to support the well-being of their teams. Leaders must role model spiritual well-being practices related to purpose, social connection, and transcendence. They must also receive training on how to appropriately support team members in their spiritual well-being in a way that respects individual differences. Workplace well-being professionals should partner with leadership development professionals, external consultants, trainers, and leadership coaches to address the special needs of leaders. Organizations can also create special leadership roles to support the development of a culture that fosters spiritual well-being.

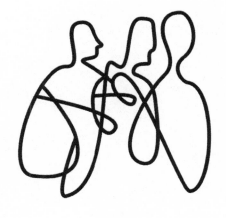

PART THREE

A Blueprint for a Best-Practices Approach

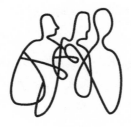

Redesigning Your Workplace Well-Being Blueprint

"A vision without a strategy remains an illusion."

— LEE BOLMAN

A Common Scenario

I step into the small meeting room, where I see my colleague, Denise, frowning over a stack of reports. Denise is one of my favorite colleagues because she's positive, fun-loving, and hard-working. Based on past experience, I know she's done all the prep needed to make this a productive meeting and that she wouldn't have asked me for a consultation if she wasn't stumped by something. I relish digging into her client's data with her and helping her identify a strategy for her upcoming year-end reporting and strategy meeting with her client.

"Hi, Denise, you look concerned about something. Is that the new culture audit report that you're piloting with your client?"

Denise glances up from the reports, with a smile. "Oh hi, Jess. Yes, this is the new report. I'm so excited to have some real client data to work with and to have this new strategic consulting tool to bring to this tough-to-please executive team. I was frowning about some of the employee responses to the open-ended comments from the survey we ran last month."

I pull up a chair alongside her and pick up the copy she's printed out for me, appreciating how she's taken time to highlight some of the more compelling data points. "That bad, huh?"

"Yeah, that bad. You know, I'm not terribly surprised because some of the health coaches working with this client's employees have been telling me about calls they're having as part of the wellness initiative. A lot of the initial call time is spent answering questions about the wellness incentive program, which penalizes employees with higher health care premiums if they don't complete at least three calls with a health coach. On subsequent calls, employees go through the motions with the coach and do only what is required so the call counts toward the incentive." Denise went on to describe how she'd advised the client to shift its incentive strategy based on the research my team had published on effective incentive designs and how she'd partnered with leaders in our call center to add training to help our coaches overcome resistance from this client's employees.

I skim over the executive summary and key data points that Denise has highlighted. "Wow, the ratings about supervisory support for employee well-being are really low. And many employees feel they can't take time to participate in well-being programs during work hours. Overtime hours are high, too. This explains the high employee stress levels we saw in the health and well-being survey earlier this year."

We continue to review the report, identifying key data points for Denise to raise in her client meeting next week, developing specific recommenda-

tions for how her client can create a more supportive, health-promoting culture. She's excited to have measurable, actionable strategies to recommend to executive leaders and data to support the underlying reasons for the dismal participation and low satisfaction rates trending on monthly reports.

When I bump into Denise the following week in the break room and ask her how the client meeting went, I learn that the client accused her of making excuses for our underperforming programs and refused to consider changing its high accountability approach using punitive incentives to encourage participation. The results of the culture audit and the comparisons between participation rates and behavior change for its organization versus other clients with a more supportive culture fell on deaf ears. They informed Denise they'd were initiating a search for a new vendor partner for well-being coaching programs for the next program cycle.

The scenario above reflects work I was doing more than a decade ago as a researcher within a national provider of workplace well-being programs for employers. Along with hypothesis testing and financial outcomes research, my team also leveraged our book of business data to support account executives in their consultation to clients. We consistently found that organizations with stronger culture of health scores had higher levels of employee well-being, higher participation rates, and better health improvement results.[236] It's a pattern I continued to uncover as I led research in a non-profit organization.[237] Application of this research to workplace spirituality undergirds the necessity of addressing well-being at the multiple levels of influence addressed in the previous chapter.

This chapter provides general guidance around how to use publicly available tools and resources to inform the design, delivery, and evaluation of workplace well-being initiatives, including those that address spiritual well-being. The US Centers for Disease Control and Prevention (CDC) provides a systematic process for developing a comprehensive, effective workplace well-being initiative including four steps: Assessment, Strategic Planning, Program Implementation, and Evaluation.[238] Each are discussed in turn below, with a focus on incorporating spiritual well-being elements into a broader well-being initiative. Whether or not your health and well-being initiatives address spiritual well-being, these steps determine the extent to which your efforts will be effective.

Assessment

The first step in a strategic approach to the design and development of workplace well-being initiatives is understanding employee needs. Assessment of employee needs can include many different types of data including employee experience surveys, employee focus group or interview data, medical and behavioral health claims, productivity and performance data, and employee health and well-being assessment data. As mentioned in a previous chapter, the Spirit at Work Survey (SAWS) is one of the most widely utilized tools for measuring spirituality needs[239] and is the only one I am aware of that measures an individual's sense of purpose, perceptions of connectivity with others, and experiences of transcendence at work. This type of survey data can be augmented by the other data types mentioned above to identify opportunities for strengthening employee well-being. Multiple data sources should be reviewed to form a complete view of individual-level needs (e.g., employee perceptions, experiences, and behaviors), interpersonal-level factors (e.g., workplace climate and team experiences), and organizational-level factors (e.g., culture audit data). This may include data from many different functional areas across the organization.

Some organizations invest heavily in a data integration strategy that allows many different data sources to be integrated at the individual level (e.g., medical claims, disability data, health assessment survey data, and workers compensation data). Even though data integration like this provides many advantages when it comes to understanding the relationships across data sources, most organizations cannot afford to invest in this level of integration. Another strategy to consider is examining all data with the same sub-population breakdowns. For example, all data might be summarized by demographic characteristics of employee, business unit, location, or job type. Overlaying the different data sources and examining how they change at these sub-population levels can reveal potentially important relationships among the data (e.g., lower employee perception scores for managers occur in units with the highest rates of disability incidence). Tracking trends over time by these same groups allow you to see how the data points move in relationship with one another.

Even though the current version (V5) does not explicitly address spiritual well-being practices, the *Health Enhancement Research Organization (HERO) Health and Well-Being Best Practices Scorecard in Collaboration with Mercer©* (HERO Scorecard) is a free web-based organizational assessment tool that can help employers identify objective, evidence-based practices to support a comprehensive, multi-level approach to workforce well-being.[240] Data are collected about what the organization is doing to invest in employee health and well-being. For example, it assesses the extent to which organizations have:

- A data-driven written strategic plan for workforce well-being with measurable objectives

- Many different types of organizational and leadership support practices related to investment, leadership behaviors, and policies
- A comprehensive approach to program offerings
- An integrated program implementation approach
- A comprehensive approach to encouraging participation
- Program measurement and evaluation strategies

Organizations can use the assessment to identify gaps in their current approach, which can inform the development of a written strategic plan.

Strategic Planning

A written strategic plan is a predictor of successful workplace well-being initiatives, but many organizations do not have a formal plan for their employee well-being programs.[241] Strategic planning includes identifying the gap between the current state of organizational support for well-being and the desired future state. Measurement tools like the HERO Scorecard, CDC Worksite Health Scorecard, and others provide expert guidance on recommended strategies and allow an organization to compare their approach with other organizations like theirs in terms of the number of employees and industry type.[242] They also provide guidance for the infrastructure needed to ensure well-being efforts are effectively supported, managed, and measured. To my knowledge, there is not a best practice assessment tool that specifically addresses workplace spirituality. This is an opportunity for those working in the workplace spirituality field, and such a resource would help translate research into practical real-world business settings.

A formal strategic plan should include the organization's reasons for investing in workforce well-being (the organization's "why"); what measurable goals and objectives it hopes to see as a result of its investment; and the specific programs, interventions, activities, and supports that will be invested in to achieve its objectives. As specifically applied to spiritual well-being, the organization should clearly articulate its reasons for incorporating the three elements discussed in this section into its broader well-being initiatives. Each of the chapters in Part Two of this book pointed to research linking workplace spirituality to business outcomes, which can inform this aspect of your strategic plan. For example, ample research on the three areas of spirituality supports a link to employee engagement in its work. Given the well-established research on the business benefits of increased employee engagement, an organization might decide to implement workplace spirituality practices. Evaluation strategies should also be included in the plan, detailing how each objective will be measured, how frequently it will be assessed, and who is accountable for data collection, monitoring, and reporting.

Once written, a strategic plan should be revisited frequently and updated as needed. Ideally, a strategic plan documents a three-year to five-year strategy and is updated annually. The plan's development and updates should include multiple stakeholders that represent different functions and leadership levels within the organization (e.g. leadership development; organizational learning; occupational health and safety; diversity, equity, and inclusion; employee assistance).

In addition to the development of a written plan, strategic planning can also include:

- Identifying senior leaders to serve as champions and role models for well-being
- Identifying a coordinator, council, or committee to manage implementation of the initiative
- Developing a budget to support planned activities
- Creating a comprehensive communication plan
- Creating a plan to support evaluation and reporting efforts
- Reviewing organizational policies that influence employee well-being

Some broad human resources policies are not explicitly health-related but have an influence on employee well-being. Policies related to diversity, equity, and inclusion (DEI); flexible scheduling, time off, breaks and working hours; professional development; supervisory behaviors; and relational dynamics may need to be created or revised so they support well-being goals and objectives. The need to address organizational policies and practices is another good reason for taking a multi-disciplinary approach and ideally, you would partner with other functional leaders to ensure employee well-being is infused into all policies.

Program Implementation

Program implementation includes mobilizing leaders to support well-being efforts, which might include providing talking points and support for leaders, so they are aware of how to communicate about and role model behaviors that support well-being efforts. This could include getting leaders involved in specific programs and sharing testimonials about how they are helpful to them. A well-integrated program implementation plan ensures a coordinated approach across different functions or departments within the organization, and a cross-sectional well-being committee can be created to represent facilities, corporate communications, human resources, organizational and leadership development, benefits, occupational health and safety, bargained labor representation, and leaders representing different facets of the organization. If there are certain types of policies that might need to be revised or created to support well-being initiatives, there needs to be an intentional plan for developing the policy, getting feedback and buy-in from stakeholders, training managers and supervisors to implement the policy, and communication strategies.

Evaluation

Ideally, evaluation strategies are detailed during the strategic planning phase and this phase executes the plan, with a focus on ensuring data are used to inform ongoing improvements to programs and processes and to bolster organizational and leadership support. For this to happen, it is necessary for multiple stakeholders to receive periodic reports about how activities are progressing, being mindful of employee feedback and identifying barriers to access or participation. Some process evaluation questions for stakeholders to consider as they are reviewing the data are the following:

- Are the individuals who most need programs and resources accessing and participating in offerings?

- Are access and participation rates at the levels needed to influence downstream outcomes and support a culture of well-being?

- How are well-being activities and programs perceived? What kind of feedback has been generated around a particular policy or program offering?

- What are the "bright spots" and success stories you're seeing?

- What are the gaps or opportunities that need to be addressed with future efforts?

- Do employees perceive the organization cares about their well-being?

- Do employees perceive their supervisor cares about their well-being?

- Do employees feel supported by their peers in pursuing their own well-being?

- Are data trending in expected directions? If not, what might be contributing to undesirable trends?

- Does new information or data need to be gathered to understand root causes for implementation issues or undesirable data trends?

- Are data trends on track to achieve expected measurable goals and objectives stated in the strategic plan?

- Is the organization realizing the value it hoped to receive as a result of the investment in well-being programs and activities?

While answering these questions is resource intense for a multi-level, comprehensive initiative, this level of attention is required to identify early when improvements or revisions to the plan are needed and to incorporate lessons learned into the implementation of future activities. Reviewing leading indicators of success along the way also informs the interpretation of downstream results. If a specific program did not meet expectations, there are upstream indicators of where things might have gotten off track.

The process evaluation questions listed above are the things you can assess in the first six to twelve months of an initiative. After that, you can add impact evaluation questions related to impacts on employee behaviors, work group climate, employee perceptions about organizational support, employee engagement in their work, and changes in specific domains of well-being (e.g., physical, mental, emotional, spiritual). Outcomes evaluation occurs two to five years following initial launch of initiatives and measures include more downstream business outcomes. What's appropriate to evaluate is dependent on the scope of the implemented well-being initiative, but common outcomes might include employee turnover rates, employee experience survey ratings, productivity and performance outcomes, and objective measures of business performance.

The US Centers for Disease Control and Prevention (CDC) provides information and tools to support workplace well-being evaluation efforts and can be used to measure and evaluate the effectiveness of many types of workplace well-being programs including those focused on spiritual well-being.[243] The Health Enhancement Research Organization (HERO) also provides guidance on employee well-being metrics that might be included in an organizational dashboard or scorecard.[244]

Special Considerations for
Spiritual Well-Being Initiatives

As you work through the steps to assess, plan, implement, and evaluate your workplace well-being efforts, you must be aware of some special considerations concerning workplace spirituality efforts. This section incorporates some cautions raised by experts and practitioners working in the workplace spirituality field over the past few decades. Those of us who are just starting to explore expanding our well-being efforts to incorporate workplace spirituality owe a debt of gratitude to the researchers, consultants, scholars, and practitioners who have identified these potential pitfalls.

Spiritual well-being can be an uncomfortable topic in the workplace due to employer concerns about the need to be inclusive of diverse perspectives, sensitive to different cultural orientations, and mindful about the potential for litigious activity associated with religious discrimination and accommodation. When implemented thoughtfully and intentionally, employers can create environments that support spiritual well-being without endorsing a specific belief system or worldview. Workplace well-being practitioners would do well to partner with diversity, equity, and inclusion (DEI) professionals to ensure spiritual well-being efforts are perceived as supportive, inclusive, and voluntary. Language matters and each organization must determine what terms and labels will be most appropriate for their organization. It can be helpful to test specific terms and language in employee focus groups or to engage members of an existing wellness champion network or advisory council.

It can also help to pilot test new programs or services with a small subset of the population before broadening their availability to the entire organization. When doing so, aim to engage a representative mix of employees from different cultural backgrounds, age groups, and levels of tenure within the organization. You may find a program element is received well among certain members of the organization but not others. Well-conducted pilot efforts communicate early and often about the experimental nature of what's being tested and engage participants in a commitment to provide candid feedback. You might also engage a pilot group specifically because members are likely to be the most critical and cynical about what is being tested. This is a useful strategy when the goal of the pilot test is to refine an offering before an official launch.

In one organization that I worked with several decades ago, we engaged a group of older male engineers, who were trained as part of their work to think critically about everything. Our initiative aimed to address interpersonal relationships and topics this group was likely to perceive as "touchy-feely." Our initial pilot test experiments with them yielded tremendously helpful feedback and insights about how specific program elements and communications would be received, and we were able to refine the elements prior to broader organizational launch. Based on the success of that early effort, we engaged the group in a one-year commitment to continue to test new concepts we were developing. They appreciated that their feedback was taken seriously, and it contributed to their perceptions of feeling valued by the organization. They also liked the idea of being part of an exclusive test group that got to receive the new stuff first.

In a different effort, we needed to pilot test short-term outcomes and the effectiveness of a training program for managers, which was delivered via distant learning to multiple sites. Pilot results would not only inform program improvements but also help us to gain buy-in from other leaders if we were able to demonstrate impressive results. For this reason, we selected pilot locations based on those who needed the training the most and who met a set of criteria that made the program more likely to succeed (e.g., plant manager support for the initiative and an onsite organizational effectiveness leader).

With most well-being initiatives, voluntariness is key. When employees feel they are being coerced or pressured to participate in something they do not want to do, it will counter what you're trying to achieve to promote employee well-being. Workplace well-being efforts have been relying on financial incentives for decades to attract employees to programs. Research shows that incentives are most useful for easy, compliance-oriented actions, such as completing a survey or getting a preventive health exam. Research is equivocal about the effectiveness of incentives on complex behaviors and especially for long-term behavior change.[245]

A strategy that seems to be effective for some organizations is group incentives that serve a broader purpose. For example, asking employees to participate in a short-term gratitude campaign with the highest participating team getting to select from a list of charities which would receive a financial contribution from the company. Voluntariness includes allowing employees to bow out of guided meditations or rituals that are embedded into team meetings. As mentioned in Chapter 7, leaders must avoid pressuring their team members to participate in spiritual well-being activities or to pressure them into disclosing information about themselves that they are not comfortable sharing. For example, employees should not be required or pressured to share a personal purpose statement with other team members.

An issue related to voluntariness is when the use of spirituality practices and beliefs causes specific groups to feel excluded. This undermines the requirements for respect and inclusion at work and threatens the well-being goals of connection and belonging.[246] What may not appear at face value to be endorsing a specific spiritual or religious doctrine could still be perceived as such. When in doubt, seek guidance from diversity, equity, and inclusion (DEI) professionals, employee resource groups, or external advisors who have implemented similar initiatives in diverse settings.

Reflective practices, such as meditation, prayer, journaling, and mindful movement, are helpful supports to many aspects of spiritual well-being, but they are less likely to occur in the face of highly compressed meeting schedules with ambitious agendas. Reflective practices require ample time be built into schedules. This is especially true when engaging in certain types of practices for the first time. Beginners often need more time to get grounded and centered in a practice, and gaining benefit from a practice can be difficult if there isn't enough time to quiet their mind of distractions. Frequent failed attempts when learning a new skill can lead to frustration. When introducing new practices, be sensitive to the needs and comfort of beginners. It can be helpful to create offerings specifically for those newer to a practice and offer separate sessions for more seasoned practitioners. It's also important to remind individuals that the word "practices" is appropriate because even seasoned veterans struggle with them. I've been working to develop a daily meditation habit for years, and I still feel like a novice when I practice.

As was discussed in Chapter 7, it's important to engage leaders early in the process of expanding their workforce well-being to include more spiritual elements. It can be helpful to engage them in dialogue about terminology and the most appropriate language to use when communicating about activities. And it's especially important that leaders experience the benefits of spiritual well-being elements for themselves. Though leaders should be allowed to bow out of practices they are uncomfortable with, identifying champions and role models from leaders is essential at all levels in the organization. If business leaders are resistant about expanding well-being efforts in this direction, more work may be needed to align the proposed plan with organizational objectives. Many organizations provide training and resources to companies in addressing purpose, connectedness, and transcendence, some of which have been identified in earlier chapters.

A final issue of concern is the risk of spiritual well-being (and any well-being initiative for that matter) being used as a management tool to manipulate employees. Communications around organizational intent for well-being initiatives should first and foremost express concern and care for employee well-being. I cringe when I see well-designed and well-intentioned initiatives communicated under the banner of a productivity and performance effort. It strips even the most thoughtfully designed initiative of its essence and authenticity. Without a genuine commitment to well-being for its own sake, employees can become cynical and resistant to engage.[247] It is especially appropriate to end with this caution as we segue into the next chapter on how an investment in whole person well-being is good for business.

CHAPTER 8

HIGHLIGHTS

- There is a four-step approach to designing and implementing effective workplace well-being initiatives including assessment, strategic planning, program implementation, and evaluation.

- Assessment includes using many different types of data collection to understand employee needs, interests, and preferences. There are numerous tools to assess employee needs related to the three elements of workplace spirituality addressed in this book.

- Many organizations lack a written strategic plan for well-being initiatives, but organizations that have them are more likely to see demonstrated impacts on employee well-being and business outcomes. There are numerous free measurement tools to support workplace well-being strategic planning and this chapter discusses the elements of a good strategic plan.

- Program implementation includes engaging stakeholders at all levels and across different functions of the organization to support well-being efforts. A collaborative, multi-disciplinary approach is necessary to develop aligned communications, policy changes, leadership training, inclusive programs and language, and cultural changes that support spiritual well-being.

- Evaluation plans should be developed as part of the strategic planning process and updated frequently to capture ongoing findings and lessons learned. A communication plan should be developed to regularly share findings with stakeholders and engage them in how to shift future strategy. These shifts should be documented in the updated strategic plan. Comprehensive evaluation includes monitoring changes in process, impact, and outcomes with free resources available to guide employers in the selection of measures and measurement tools.

- Discussions about elements of workplace spirituality must be inclusive of diverse perspectives, faith traditions, and world views. Employers must foster cultures that support spiritual well-being without endorsing a specific belief system. All offerings must be perceived as voluntary.

- Though research supports strong business benefits related to workplace spirituality, it is critical to approach such efforts with an employee-centric approach. Hidden agendas related to corporate profitability invites cynicism and diminishes employee trust and engagement.

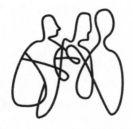

CHAPTER 9

Whole Person Well-Being Is Better for Business

"Engaging the hearts, minds, and hands of talent
is the most sustainable source of competitive advantage."

— GREG HARRIS

My Best Self

Even though I don't have any meetings on my calendar, I wake up early without an alarm. It's still dark outside as I roll over to glance at the clock on my bedside table. It's 5 a.m., and I have the whole day ahead of me without a single disruption on my calendar. It's a surprising rarity. Friends and family are often amazed when I tell them how many calls I have every week even though I'm taking a year off from paid work to re-examine my professional work and explore a potential shift in focus. Doing so required substantial effort to support my previous organization in the transition to replace me and to wrap up several large collaborative research projects.

Sensing a deep need for rest, earlier in the year, I decided to clear my schedule of all commitments and go "off the grid" for nearly two months. I even canceled my weekly call with my twin sister and stopped attending weekly video conference calls with my community cohort from church. COVID-19 rates were high at that time, and most of the state was in lockdown, so the only things to do were recreational activities outdoors and going grocery shopping. Even the beaches and parks were closed during this time, so I was largely confined to my home. I spent that time indulging in restorative practices and reading whatever I had the desire to read. I slept in as late as my body wanted, did yoga and strength workouts, practiced meditation, and journaled. After breakfast and a shower, I read for a few hours and then went for a mindful two-and-a-half mile walk around my neighborhood. Depending on how early I had gotten up, I might have read some more and gone for another walk with my spouse before dinner. After dinner I might have read some more.

After three weeks of observing this schedule, my head was full of many thoughts from the reading I was doing, and I decided to re-engage in social phone calls with my sister and a few close friends. I discovered that even an introvert like me needed the benefit of dialogue partners to process the ideas bouncing around in my head. Especially because the ideas had to do with the deep inner work of revising my life purpose and considering the future direction of my professional work.

This kind of reflection and the desire for a long break from the constant demands of my work as a researcher was why I wanted to take some significant time away from work. At the end of my self-imposed "off the grid" period, I decided to explore shifting my professional work focus to spiritual well-being and spent much of the year familiarizing myself with the research. As COVID-19 restrictions eased, we were able to do some cautious traveling and I was engaged in several months of part-time consulting work, which helped pay for the travel. That included a "bucket list" pilgrimage hike of the Camino de Santiago de Compostela in northern Spain for several weeks, which ended with my decision to take the plunge and write a book.

Most mornings, I am out of bed by 5:30 a.m. without an alarm clock, and I have maintained the rhythm established during my "off the grid" experiment. The morning block of yoga, workout, meditation, and journaling comprises roughly three hours of "temple time." It's the non-negotiable daily investment that I make to my physical, mental, and spiritual well-being. Even while vacationing, I maintained at least ninety minutes of my coveted "temple time." The practices ground me and prepare me for the day ahead, allowing me to approach whatever surfaces with a more open disposition and the ability to pause and reflect before I respond.

I try to be in my writing chair by nine a.m. each day to read and write for a total of four to six hours, depending on disruptions from scheduled calls with professional peers, mentors, and subject matter experts who serve as sounding boards during this writing process or who are part of the small inner circle that I keep in regular contact with during this year of exploration. I've been trying to maintain a midday mindful walk, which I try to do in silence. No calls, music, or podcasts. Just reflective time that often surfaces appreciation for the landscape around me, inter-cessory prayer for loved ones, and rumination about what I'm reading or writing about. Some days, I decide to do my walk during a call or don't fit a walk in until the end of the day before dinner. In a few short weeks, this pattern will come to an end as I return to work commitments and the need to balance my continued study and spiritual well-being practices. My intention is to maintain my version of "temple time" and continue with mindful walks a few times a week, but I honestly don't know what the rigors and demands of returning to full-time work will allow. I'm thankful for the time that I've had to discover and practice what it feels like to be well rested, fully engaged, and balanced across the domains of physical, mental, and spiritual well-being. It feels like my best self and it's a treasure I won't easily relinquish.

I recognize that the journey I've traveled to more fully develop spiritual well-being practices into my work and life represents a single case study. My experience of feeling more energized, fulfilled, and happy as a result of this more holistic approach to my well-being may not extend to everyone who engages in similar practices, but a growing body of research supports the link among workplace spirituality, individual well-being, and workplace performance. That's why we must rely on research to guide our way as we develop workplace spirituality initiatives directed at whole populations of employees. It can inform what kinds of programs or organizational supports to incorporate and help us understand what kinds of outcomes might be yielded. Research can also guide our evaluation of workplace spirituality initiatives.

A Word of Caution

Thus far, I've woven research supporting my recommendations into discussion about some of the practices and elements of spiritual well-being. This chapter aims to address the business case for including spiritual well-being into a comprehensive approach to worker well-being. Even though research on workplace spirituality has grown significantly in the past fifteen years, it's an emerging field of study and one I'm still seeking to fully familiarize myself with as I write this book. Inconsistencies continue to abound in how spirituality is defined and measured.

You will find a dearth of well-designed research studies on spirituality interventions in real-world business settings, and the diversity of methodological approaches used across existing studies confound the ability to make sweeping statements about what is most effective. Moreover, when a study finds a particular intervention approach was effective or ineffective, it may be generalizable only to that intervention in the representative population. In other words, if a mindfulness intervention helped older, female nurses manage their stress, then that specific intervention may be useful in helping older, female nurses in other organizations. But the same program may not be as effective for younger males in grocery stores. Similar results may not be observed from a different mindfulness program in the same setting. Therefore, testing interventions in a multitude of real-world occupational settings are important for the growth of these types of programs. There is a critical need for program providers, well-being practitioners, and employers to invest in quality program evaluations and to share them with others. Workplace spirituality abounds with case studies, but most of them are not subjected to peer review or grounded in a level of rigor that would merit publication in scientific journals.

Once there are enough studies to evaluate a body of research, we can use systematic literature reviews and meta-analysis studies to determine if more generalized statements about program effectiveness are merited. This chapter does not aim to provide a systematic, exhaustive review of the entire body of evidence that exists in the workplace spirituality field. Researchers who have spent their entire careers in this area of study will likely identify important studies that I've missed. I welcome their outreach so I can continue my own journey of discovering the knowledge base that exists. In the meantime, I'm sharing what I've learned from researchers who have been pursuing this area of study. The studies are grouped in descending order from the most robust and generalizable approaches to less robust approaches.

Meta-Analysis Studies and Systematic Reviews

Meta-analysis studies use data analysis techniques to combine the results from multiple studies into a single set of findings or conclusions. They require all studies to use the same research question and similar research study methods. An overly precise set of criteria for study inclusion and methodological precision can limit the number of studies used in an analysis, but it strengthens the quality of study findings.

A systematic research review is similarly rigorous but does not attempt to pool data from across the various studies into a single statistical analysis. Instead, it seeks to draw a set of generalizable conclusions about the focused research question.

The initial management journal articles on workplace spirituality emerged in the mid-1990s, and they largely focused on conceptual approaches to measuring and defining spirituality. This line of research continues today, with no consensus definition or measurement tools. Some have argued against the development of a single consensus definition or measurement approach, recommending researchers select the tools that measure the specific dimensions or aspects of spirituality applying to their study or are most culturally appropriate for the population being studied.

A 2016 systematic review of published research[248] confirmed an earlier conclusion by other researchers[249] that most definitions of workplace spirituality include the dimensions of inner life, meaningful work, and a sense of community. These reviews and my own discovery process informed the approach I am proposing for spiritual well-being in this book. Forniciari and Lund are credited with conducting the first meta-analysis study of workplace spirituality approaches and found none of the 231 peer-reviewed studies in their sample addressed workplace outcomes other than stress.[250]

One of the first reviews to provide information about individual and organizational outcomes marked a shift toward more quantitative measurement approaches and the influence of workplace spirituality on employee attitudes, performance, and ethical decision making.[251] Key findings were a positive influence of workplace spirituality on

- Job commitment, satisfaction, and performance
- Altruism and conscientiousness
- Self-career management
- Reduced inter-role conflict
- Reduced frustration
- Organization-based self-esteem
- Employee involvement
- Employee retention
- Ethical individual and organizational behavior

A more recent meta-analysis was isolated to only six randomized controlled trials that compared the effectiveness of spiritual interventions to controls, finding employees in the intervention group improved health outcomes to a significantly greater degree than employees in the comparison group.[252] The majority of the studies focused on different forms of yoga as the primary intervention, finding positive individual outcomes, such as lower levels of emotional exhaustion, lower rates of stress, better well-being, lower back pain, and better job satisfaction. The meta-analysis portion of the study focused only on the interventions using yoga and assessed the overall impact on stress. This resulted in a pooled sample across four studies, with the finding of a positive impact on stress, confirming the findings of other researchers who had published a previous meta-analysis of workplace yoga interventions.[253] The fact that only six studies could be included from an initial pool of 2,832 studies supports the authors' conclusion that the use of diverse methods makes generalizations about health outcomes associated with workplace spirituality interventions challenging.

Empirical Literature Reviews

When a body of research shows a lot of variation, referencing well-conducted literature reviews will help gain an understanding of what is known about the effectiveness of certain interventions. Empirical literature reviews differ from systematic reviews in that they allow for some variation in the nature of the research questions answered and in study methods.

Two published literature reviews reported a positive relationship between workplace spirituality and organizational commitment, job satisfaction, employee productivity, and various measures of performance.[254] Specific studies point to the role of workplace spirituality as a contributor to positive interpersonal relationship behaviors including altruism, conscientiousness, reduced inter-role conflict, reduced frustration, and ethical behavior. Such changes in interpersonal relationship behaviors may have been drivers of the business outcomes identified in these literature reviews. These findings have been reported using multiple measures of workplace spirituality across employee populations in Brazil, China, India, Iran, Malaysia, Pakistan, Taiwan, and the United States.

A systematic review by Harold Koenig provides an exceptionally thorough review of empirical and clinical research studies linking measures of spirituality and religion with health and well-being. Given the established links between employee health and well-being and business-relevant measures, such as employee productivity and performance along with health care utilization and costs, this body of research contributes a richer understanding of the potential value of workplace spirituality.

Space does not allow for the full detail of the rich findings reported in Koenig's review, so this summary focuses on only the most robust methodological studies of health and well-being outcomes associated with spirituality and religion. This is possible because a single researcher consistently rated the methodological rigor of all studies included in the review and grouped reported results categorically by level of study rigor. It's a massive and commendable undertaking![255]

My one wish as a consumer of Koenig's research is that the findings were organized based on how higher levels of spirituality and/or religion were defined and measured. Though commendable, the review summarizes all findings as an amalgamation of all studies that assessed the influence of spirituality or religion on study outcomes, which makes it difficult to tease apart the findings focused only on the three aspects of spirituality I focus on in this book (cultivating a culture of purpose, connectedness/belonging, and transcendence). That caveat aside, according to the review, higher levels of spirituality and/or religion are associated with the following:

- Coping with a wide range of medical illnesses

- Positive emotions such as well-being, happiness, hope, optimism, meaning and purpose, high self-esteem, and a sense of control over life

  o Of 120 studies, 82% reported a positive relationship with well-being and happiness

  o Of 6 studies, 50% reported a positive relationship with hope

  o Of 11 studies, 73% reported a positive relationship with optimism

  o Of 42 studies, 81% reported a positive relationship with meaning and purpose

  o Of 25 studies, 68% reported a positive relationship with self-esteem

  o Of 9 studies, 44% reported a positive relationship with sense of control

  o Of 20 studies, 75% reported a positive relationship with altruism and volunteering

  o Of 10 studies, 70% reported a positive relationship with forgiveness of others

- Lower levels of depression

  o Of 70 prospective cohort studies, 56% reported greater spirituality was associated with lower levels of depression

  o Of 30 clinical trials, 63% found spirituality and religion interventions produced better depression outcomes

- Lower levels of suicide or suicide attempts

- Lower levels of anxiety

- Lower alcohol use, abuse, or dependence

- Higher levels of social support

- Lower rates of cigarette smoking

- A healthier diet

- Lower incidence of coronary heart disease

- Lower incidence of hypertension

- Lower incidence of dementia

- Higher levels of immune function

- Higher levels of physical function

- Higher levels of self-rated health

- Lower levels of pain or somatic symptoms

- Greater length of life (lower mortality)

Explanatory Pathways

Although the more systematic reviews mentioned above provide strong support for the positive influence of workplace spirituality offerings on business-relevant outcomes, practitioners are typically more interested in understanding predictive pathways that can help us identify short-term and long-term measures of impact. Structural equation modeling is a data analysis technique often used to understand such pathways.

A 2014 study of a random sample of employees working in numerous state-owned banks in Iran used a structural equation modeling approach to better understand the pathway of outcomes from workplace spirituality to organizational citizenship behaviors. Their measure of workplace spirituality was comprised of three dimensions including meaningful work, sense of community, and alignment of values. All were strongly associated with workplace spirituality. Employees with stronger levels of workplace spirituality were more likely to exhibit positive organizational citizenship behaviors including conscientiousness, sportsmanship, civic virtue, courtesy, and altruism.

A later study used structural equation modeling with a population of nurses from three hospitals in Malaysia to understand predictors of turnover, finding that nurses with higher levels of workplace spirituality were less likely to report intention to leave the organization. Specific contributors to this relationship include nurses finding their duties meaningful, having better relationships with colleagues, and feeling alignment with organizational values. Workplace spirituality also predicted greater levels of organizational citizenship behavior, which improved job satisfaction and service quality to patients.

These early findings are encouraging, meriting further consideration of workplace spirituality as a worthwhile investment for business. While I maintain that organizations would be best served to invest in whole person well-being approaches because they will best serve their employees, it strengthens stakeholder buy-in to know evidence supports the common refrain that employee well-being is good for business.

The next chapter specifically addresses how you can engage stakeholders in your organization by using a storytelling approach to align the potential benefits associated with workplace spirituality, the specific strategies your organization decides to implement, and the results observed from implemented programs.

CHAPTER 9

HIGHLIGHTS

- All of the practices recommended in this book are supported by research; however, the scientific evidence base for workplace spirituality is still emerging. Pilot testing, a phased approach, and employee involvement in the development and implementation of workplace spirituality offerings is recommended.

- Workplace spirituality is linked with positive changes in job commitment, job satisfaction and performance; altruism and conscientiousness; self-career management; better working relationships; employee engagement and retention; and more ethical employee behavior.

- Specific workplace spirituality interventions associated with the most robust research support include yoga, mindfulness, and purpose interventions.

- Higher levels of spirituality are linked with healthier self-care behaviors, better physical health outcomes, clinical outcomes and longevity, positive emotional well-being, mental well-being, and social well-being.

CHAPTER 10

Aligning Vision, Solution, and Results

"Not only do we understand the world through stories,
but we understand ourselves through stories.
And the stories we tell about our lives become our lives."

— CHARLES VOGL

Crafting Your Story

I've opened each chapter of this book with my own personal story about how work has been a positive or a challenging influence on my well-being. Given the nature of this book, it made sense to include my spiritual well-being journey. This was not an easy decision. It would have been far more comfortable for me to draw upon published case examples about organizations that have been incorporating spiritual well-being elements into how work gets done (e.g., Aetna, Ascension Health, Eileen Fisher, Ford Motor Company, The Body Shop, Tom's of Maine). Though that would have felt safer, telling my story allows me to role model the vulnerability and authenticity needed to create workplace cultures that invite a whole-person approach to well-being.

Before we can hope to inspire change and create a workplace culture that fosters purpose, connection, and transcendence, we need to check in with our own well-being journey. How are we incorporating spiritual well-being practices into our own lives? How willing are we to share with others what's been most helpful or meaningful in our journey? Every person's journey differs and so the sharing isn't intended to influence others to walk the same path but rather to create an environment where people feel comfortable bringing these aspects of their well-being into the workplace. Creating new norms within the workplace takes time but it starts with a small handful of courageous people willing to talk about their purpose in life, being willing to bring their more authentic selves into everyday interactions with their co-workers, and willing to share their stories about where they have encountered awe, beauty, and wonder in their lives.

Research on mirror neurons indicates that hearing a well-told story about a self-transcendent experience can inspire well-being in others. The sudden plunge into predominantly digital interactions during the COVID-19 pandemic were a catalyst to a more fulsome view into one another's lives. We suddenly saw pets and family members showing up on video calls. They were moments of delight for me! Engaging with colleagues from our home environments created an opening for more vulnerable and authentic conversations. Then our awareness of racial injustice invited another deeper layer of dialogue. We unpacked uncomfortable discoveries revealed when we considered how societal and workplace systems contributed to privileges not equally accessible to all our peers. Workplace conversations delved into issues of implicit bias and created space for new narratives focused on healing. Much of this work involved inviting one another to share our stories.

A movement is growing around storytelling as we discover the power of shared narratives to guide collective decision making, make mean-

ing, and navigate the circumstances of our daily lives as they unfold.[256] Sharing our stories with one another can also be a pathway to stronger, more genuine connections at work, breaking down barriers, helping us to develop empathy for one another, and contributing to our own physical, mental, and emotional well-being.[257] As we collectively share our unfolding stories, we can co-create a new shared story about what it means to experience deeper purpose, richer connections, and self-transcendent moments within the world of our work.

Each organization that chooses to walk this courageous journey of fostering spiritual well-being at work serves as an inspiration to other organizations that might prefer to follow the well-worn path rather than blaze their own trail. As you consider where you are on your personal journey and where your organization is on its journey, I invite you to imagine the story you'd like to tell someday. Envision what it looks like for you and your organization to thrive. What about your story would be helpful and inspiring to others? How would sharing your story or your organization's story benefit you or the organization? Consider what attitudes and behaviors need to shift to achieve your vision. Compare and contrast the gap between what is and what might be. Now, how can you be the bridge that connects the dots between current state and future vision? Who might be willing to come alongside you in building the bridge? What steps might you or others take to break new ground in your well-being efforts?

Inspiring Others to Join You on the Journey

Inspiring others to come alongside and co-create a new way of showing up and interacting in the world of work may need to begin by sharing the evidence demonstrating how a spiritual well-being approach can support individual, team, or organizational objectives. Chapter 9 provided some high-level evidence on the knowledge-base and you might want to draw from it to customize your business case. Additional supporting evidence was included in Chapters 4 through 6 on the three elements of spiritual well-being.

Consider the pain points that exist within your organization and which elements of a spiritual well-being approach might resonate most strongly. But remember that statistics and data will almost certainly prove insufficient to shift a mindset or approach. Nobel Prize winner Daniel Kahneman once observed, "No one ever made a decision because of a number. They need a story."[258] What are the organizational stories that form the architectural bones of your case for change? How does your organization's data add flesh to those bones? Can you identify individual testimonials that humanize and put a face to the body of evidence? And how might your own story contribute?

Award-winning filmmaker and author Charles Vogl offers guidance to leaders on crafting a compelling personal story in his book, *Storytelling for Leaders:*[259]

- Tell the truth of your story as you remember it, making corrections if information surfaces that seems to conflict with your memory.

- Share with intention by identifying the point of your story. The point of the story is what you hope to achieve because of sharing it. Are you hoping to inspire listeners to act or to support your well-being efforts in a new way? Write the point of your story and practice telling your story in a way that focuses on your intention for sharing it, cutting out extraneous detail.

- Refine your language and the details of your story for your audience. Remove lingo or jargon they won't understand. Consider the terms that will most resonate with your audience and adjust your language for different audiences if necessary. Incorporate examples that reflect their role or the challenges they face. Share the level of detail most appropriate for your audience. If you are not sure how to do this, recruit a member from your target audience to listen to your story and help you refine the language or terms you use.

- Even as you share your story, know that others will interpret it differently, gleaning different lessons from it. This is an opportunity to gain new insights about how your story is received and identify opportunities to refine how you tell it or to simply be more sensitive to others' point of view and mindful of your story's influence on others.

Keep in mind that a balanced approach is needed. Many of your stakeholders and potential collaborators may require that you start with hard, quantitative data. Stories complement quantitative data, allowing us to form a more emotional connection. A story arc might look something like this:

- Start with intention by sharing organizational data about a specific pain point or challenge (e.g., turnover rates, burnout data, employee pulse survey data). This gets attention. Alternatively, share data that emphasize a bright spot or an exceptionally positive result.

- Humanize the quantitative data with qualitative data (e.g., how the data point translated into a specific client or patient testimonial, a comment made during an employee exit interview, or a comment posted on Glassdoor). This surfaces emotion, creating connection. Aim to generate feelings of concern, compassion, inspiration, or hope.

- Share evidence on how elements of a spiritual well-being approach (purpose, connection, self-transcendence) can address or support the data point. This offers a potential new solution to an existing problem or reinforces what's going right in a solution you've recently implemented.

- Share a story of what another company is doing or has done to incorporate the spiritual well-being approach (this may require benchmarking what another leading employer has done). This offers inspiration, another emotive response.

- Close with what is at stake for the organization and propose a specific call to action (e.g., creating a small cross-functional working group to develop a more specific proposal with next steps).

- Reinforce the need for a people-centric approach. Close with an appeal to the heart. This requires you to engage your listeners' emotions or incite them to feel differently. Incorporating a brief but moving testimonial about a challenge that you or someone in the organization has experienced and how that challenge was overcome is one way to appeal to the heart.

Can you see the dance between head and heart in the story arc above? We are not aiming to be maniacally manipulative with this approach but rather we want to more fully engage the brain centers focused on analytics and logic as well as the brain centers focused on feelings and intuition. Such balanced arguments are the stuff of action, forward movement, and transformational change.

Setting Realistic Expectations

One of the biggest challenges to overcome when you are selling a new idea or approach is to balance the need to inspire, by using exemplar case stories, with the reality of how your organization is likely to take action. I've observed this in my previous work as an outcomes researcher, where a best-in-class customer example is shared to inspire others to shift their approach. An organization might be moved to agree that a changed approach is necessary but may not be willing to invest to the same degree represented in the best-in-class example.

Once an organization has indicated what or how it is willing to invest to move forward, that's the time to set realistic expectations about what kinds of outcomes an organization will likely see. Consider the examples of the multi-level approach to fostering a culture of purpose provided in Chapter 4 and the outcomes observed as a result of their efforts. If your organization were to offer one element of the multi-level approach (e.g., a single workshop on purpose for employees or a one-time, eight-week purpose challenge), your organization cannot expect to realize the same results yielded by organizations using a multi-level approach with many different elements.

I sometimes see big shifts in strategy occur after a new initiative has been launched. The organization may have developed a robust written strategic plan with measurable goals and objectives. Senior leadership support was granted along with an operating budget. Midway through implementation, a seismic shift occurred (e.g., there was a downturn in the economy, or a global pandemic mandated a shift to remote work arrangements). It's important to document any shifts that were made in the evolving strategic planning document and to engage stakeholders around modifying expectations for measurable objectives stated in the plan. Documenting the reason for a change in plans becomes part of the well-being story arc. It can be presented as a challenge that had to be overcome or as a lesson learned. A growth mindset approach is key to interpretation of disappointing results. It's not the result that matters but what you do with that information over the long-term that counts.

Co-Creating the New Narrative

In Chapter 8, we discussed the importance of evaluating the fruits of your well-being efforts as you are implementing them. We often start with a vision for our best-case scenario. Sometimes our wildest expectations are exceeded. For example, a small pilot effort is met with extraordinary enthusiasm. Participation was so robust that waiting lists had to be created or new resources had to be invested or mobilized to meet unexpected levels of demand. Other times, we encounter challenges that require creativity and problem solving.

Avoid the temptation to create solutions on your own. Engage as many of your stakeholders as you can in deciding the path forward in the face of new, unexpected challenges. Revisit the vision and intentions for your effort and imagine together how certain decisions will influence the story you will be able to tell about your well-being efforts. If you developed guiding principles or have a set of shared values to help guide decision making, be sure to pause and refer to them before making a final decision about how to move forward. This reconnection with the organization's story of a hoped-for future may help you and other organizational decision makers take a more people-centric approach.

Closing Thoughts

When you pick up a new book and consider whether you will read it, what informs your decision to buy it and invest the time? Perhaps you picked up this book because you are hungry for change, sensing that your organization's approach to well-being isn't meeting the deeper needs of those it aims to serve.

If you are engaged in full-time work, you, your colleagues, and those you lead spend more than a third of your lives interacting with the world of work. What is the influence of that exposure? Is the workplace an agent of positive flourishing or a threat to well-being that must be endured and recovered from at the end of each day?

At our core, each one of us is wired to make meaning out of the circumstances of our lives, to feel a sense of belonging and connection to those around us, and to find inspiration in contributing to something greater than ourselves in the company of others. A fundamental part of being human is to desire such things, and the workplace has a tremendous opportunity to support each one of us in our pursuit of purpose, connection, and self-transcendence.

Though workplace spirituality is an emerging field, an evidence base exists to guide us on how to create a workplace culture that supports a richer, more holistic approach to well-being. A systemic, strategic approach is needed, not a set of programmatic tactics that serve as window dressing to "check the box" on competitive benefits.

There is an opportunity to bring together multiple disciplines to create a more enticing workplace culture that attracts top talent, protects high performers from burnout, and mobilizes teams to support one another's growth while meeting performance standards. Reimagining workplace well-being requires the collaboration of stakeholders from benefits; human resources; diversity, equity, and inclusion (DEI); organizational learning and development; facilities management; corporate social responsibility; risk management; and occupational health and safety. And all levels of leadership have a role to play in transforming the workplace culture into one grounded in the understanding that human flourishing is what drives bottom line business performance and sustainable flourishing for our world.

As you consider the weight of the evidence in support of workplace spirituality and the nature of the challenges before you as an individual, a team member, a leader, a member of society, what next step is stirring within you? How do you feel called to make a positive difference in your own life and in the lives of others by applying this information to your practice of well-being? The path lays before you and it is up to you to begin writing the next chapter of your story and consider how you might influence your organization's approach to well-being.

HIGHLIGHTS

- Fostering a culture of purpose, connection, and transcendence begins by activating employees at all levels in the organization in discussions about what matters most to them.

- Individual storytelling supports the identification of shared purpose, values, and desired ways of relating to one another at work. Storytelling can be a catalyst for creating stronger relationships, more authentic ways of communicating, and trust.

- The collective sharing of individual stories by employees at all levels of the organization can help co-create a new shared story about what it means to experience deeper purpose, richer connections, and self-transcendent moments within the world of work.

- Storytelling can help engage stakeholders across the organization to support well-being efforts because stories engage the heart and inspire others. Storytelling complemented with research and data engages the head and the heart.

- Every organization's well-being journey is constantly unfolding and evolving. So, stories about what we hoped to achieve, how we went about meeting our goals, what we learned along the way, and how we adjusted our approach are important contexts for expectation setting around outcomes. All future planning is grounded in an organization's historical journey because you can't move forward effectively until you know where you've been.

- Engage employees at all levels of the organization to envision your approach to workplace spirituality and well-being. Case stories from other organizations can be inspiring, but each organization must co-create its own vision and approach to employee well-being.

- A robust evidence base exists to guide us on how to create a workplace culture that supports a more holistic approach to employee well-being. It requires a strategic, systemic approach rather than a loose set of unaligned programmatic tactics.

- Effective workplace well-being approaches include addressing the spiritual elements of purpose, connection, and transcendence. Reimagining workplace well-being requires multi-disciplinary collaboration with the support of leaders at all levels within the organization.

- When done well, workplace spirituality can create a more enticing workplace culture that attracts top talent, protects high performers from burnout, and mobilizes teams to support one another's growth and well-being while meeting performance standards.

Jessica Grossmeier

Jessica Grossmeier, PhD, MPH, is a workplace well-being thought leader with more than twenty-five years of experience advancing individual and population health. Serving the past 20 years as an outcomes researcher and program evaluation consultant, Dr. Grossmeier has executed research studies demonstrating health and financial outcomes for workplace well-being initiatives sponsored by numerous large, national employers. More recently, her research has focused on identifying best practice approaches to workplace well-being initiatives that are associated with superior health and business outcomes. Dr. Grossmeier has published more than eighty articles in peer-reviewed and industry professional journals and presented at more than 100 industry events and webinars.

Dr. Grossmeier currently advises employers and those who serve their workplace well-being needs on evidence-based approaches to workplace well-being initiatives and program evaluation. She also enjoys sharing her expertise by mentoring mid-level career professionals, speaking at industry national conferences, and serving on industry advisory boards.

Jessica lives in the Bay Area of California where she enjoys hiking and biking adventures with her high school sweetheart and husband of more than twenty-five years. Other interests include yoga, reading, healthy gourmet cooking, wine tasting, and practicing the art of gathering with family and friends.

She welcomes you to contact her with your questions or response to this book. You can find her contact information and follow her work at http://www.JessicaGrossmeier.com.

Additional Resources

The organizations listed below represent organizations that provide free information and resources that are evidence-based and explore a multi-disciplinary approach to spirituality. Though some of the organizations were founded by individuals observing a specific faith tradition, all encourage the exchange of information that fosters connection, meaning and purpose, and a life of spiritual growth. These organizations augment the many resources cited within the previous chapters.

Academy of Management (AOM) – Management, Spirituality & Religion (MSR) Community

MSR is an interest group organized under the auspices of the Academy of Management (AOM). MSR's mission is to encourage the discovery, dissemination, and application of knowledge about the relationship between management, spirituality, and religion. The community provides numerous opportunities for collaboration and connection through its ongoing events and communications. For more information: www.msr.aom.org/home.

Fetzer Institute

The Fetzer Institute is a foundation that uses philanthropic resources to build the spiritual foundation for a loving world. It funds innovators and organizations that research spirituality, engage in individual and societal spiritual transformation, and build a spiritual infrastructure for the future. Organizational Culture is one of its current program areas. Based in Michigan, The Fetzer Institute operates two retreat centers. For more information: www.fetzer.org.

Global Dharma Center

The Global Dharma Center is a US-based non-sectarian, non-profit corporation that aims to inspire and empower people from all cultures to live and work from a spiritual basis. It offers research, publications, training, and other free services. Resources include a spiritual-based leadership research program and a searchable knowledge-base of executive interviews. For more information: www.globaldharma.org/index.htm.

Greater Good Science Center

The Greater Good Science Center at UC Berkeley conducts interdisciplinary research on the science of inner and interpersonal peace. It also disseminates practical, research-supported education to parents, teachers, and practitioners to apply research to personal and professional practice. The Center also publishes *Greater Good Magazine* to disseminate emerging research on compassion, happiness, and altruism. Its many activities include blogs, seminars, institutes, and online courses to make the science of meaningful life accessible and practical to the general public. For more information: www.ggsc.berkeley.edu.

International Institute for Spiritual Leadership

The International Institute for Spiritual Leadership serves leaders and organizations seeking new leadership models, with a commitment to co-creating a conscious, flourishing world that works for everyone. Though it does provide consulting services and executive assessment and coaching, numerous free resources include peer-reviewed published research articles and videos. For more information: www.iispiritual leadership.com.

John Templeton Foundation

The John Templeton Foundation was established in 1987 and began funding general research in 1992 to understand the work and purpose of the Creator, study and stimulate progress in religion, and research the benefits of religion. Numerous white papers are available on the organization's website. Templeton Press was established in 1997 with a focus on books that promote a deeper understanding of the influence of spirituality, beliefs, and values on human health, happiness, and prosperity. For more information: www.templeton .org/about.

On Being Project

The On Being Project is a non-profit media and public life initiative that explores the intersection of spiritual inquiry, science, social healing, and the arts. Its services include a public radio show, podcasts, and online tools for "the art of living," including the newly launched Wisdom App. For more information: www.onbeing.org.

Tyson Center for Faith and Spirituality

The Tyson Center for Faith and Spirituality brings together thought leaders and business executives to promote scholarship on the impact of faith and spirituality in the workplace. Its three strategic focus areas include education, business and community outreach, and research. For more information: www.tfsw.uark.edu/sbl/overview.php.

Acknowledgments

This book might never have been written without the extraordinary encouragement and support of my husband, Chris, who allowed me the great luxury of a sabbatical year devoted to following the breadcrumbs of my curiosity. My constant companion, dialogue partner, and provider of much tangible support from exploration to discovery to commitment to execution, he is my most frequent mention in my daily gratitude journal. And also my coffee barista, chief technology officer, website designer, and best friend. There is no one I'd rather have beside me on this journey.

Several friends provided unique forms of encouragement and support, especially Kim Thomson Gaffney, Rose Iris Reintar Rehrig, and Laura Topor. A special thanks to Laura for encouraging me to "just take a leap of faith and do something" after many months of listening to me waffle about the decision to write a book and to Rose and Kim for giving me the courage to be more authentic and vulnerable in my writing. Much appreciation also goes to my twin sister, Rhea Fix, for her steadfast support as my weekly dialogue partner and to my spiritual sabbatical mentor, Andrea Anderson.

Then there are the professional peers who so generously listened to my ideas, asked better questions, challenged my thinking, shared resources, read early drafts, and walked alongside me in countless intangible ways. Some of this book's content also draws upon their expertise: Jack Bastable, Dr. Jack Groppel, Brandon Peele, Dr. Renee Moorefield, Laura Putnam, Dr. Michelle Segar, Dr. Victor J. Strecher,

Dr. Paul Terry, Charles Vogl, and Eric Zimmerman. I also drew heavily from the work of Dr. Jim Loehr and Dr. Judi Neal. Special thanks to Dr. Victor J. Strecher for writing the foreword and for his tireless work to help others identify their life purpose.

A special thanks to Michelle Railton, Newton Cheng, and Angela Sherry at Google for inviting me to participate in the Google Community Campfire experiment featured in Chapter 5. The experience changed my life by forging new friendships and sparking professional support and collaboration.

Numerous additional thought leaders and researchers contributed substantially to my foundational knowledge of the factors that foster a culture of workplace well-being, including Dr. David Anderson, Dr. Ron Goetzel, Dr. Wendy Lynch, Dr. Tre' McCalister, Dr. Steven Noeldner, Dr. Ken Pelletier, and Dr. Seth Serxner.

The world of book publishing is often overwhelming for first-time writers, and I owe a debt of gratitude to Catherine Gregory and Nathan Joblin at Modern Wisdom Press for making the journey much less arduous than I'd imagined. They held my hand from ideation to writing to editing to design to marketing and book launch. Special thanks to Brandon Peele for introducing me to Catherine.

With Appreciation

This book was written for those who strive to make the world of work a place where people can bring their most authentic selves, where they can inspire and be inspired by others, and where they can contribute meaningfully to a better planet.

As a special thanks for purchasing this book, please go to my website for special bonus materials only available to readers of this book.

For More Resources Visit:
http://www.JessicaGrossmeier.com

When prompted, please enter the following Access Code:
TRANSCEND

Notes

1   Victor J Strecher, personal communication.

2   Grossmeier, J. 2019. "Addressing spiritual well-being in the workplace." *American Journal of Health Promotion* 33 (7): 1081–1093.

3   US Bureau of Labor Statistics. 2021. *JOLTS Data.* December 8. Accessed December 14, 2021. https://www.bls.gov/news.release/jolts.nr0.htm.

4   Dina Bass. March 16, 2022. "More young workers are considering leaving your company: survey." Bloomberg Technology. Accessed March 31, 2022. https://www.bloomberg.com/news/articles/2022-03-16/the-great-resignation-may-be-accelerating-microsoft-s-global-survey-shows.

5   Leong, Lisa, Monique Ross, and Maria Tickle. 2021. "Here comes the Great Resignation. Why millions of employees could quit their jobs post-pandemic." *ABC Radio National News.* September 23. Accessed December 14, 2021. https://www.abc.net.au/news/2021-09-24/the-great-resignation-post-pandemic-work-life-balance/100478866.

6   Hsu, Andrea. 2021. "As the pandemic recedes, millions of workers are saying 'I quit'." *NPR.* June 24. Accessed December 14, 2021. https://www.npr.org/2021/06/24/1007914455/as-the-pandemic-recedes-millions-of-workers-are-saying-i-quit.

7   Visier, Inc. 2021. "When vacations aren't enough: New Visier survey finds 70% of burnt out workers would leave current job." *Outsmart.* Accessed December 14, 2021. https://www.visier.com/blog/trends/new-survey-70-percent-burnt-out-employees-would-leave-current-job.

8   Maslach, C. 1993. "Burnout: A multidimensional perspective." In *Professional Burnout: Recent Developments in Theory and Research*, by W B Schaufeli, C Maslach and T Marek, 19–32. Taylor & Francis.

9   Doniger, Alicia. 2021. "The future of work is here, employee burnout needs to go." *CNBC Workforce Wire.* September 23. Accessed December 14, 2021; Bika, Nikoletta. 2021. "Employee burnout for employers: costs, causes and cures." *Workable Stories & Insights.* Accessed December 14, 2021. https://resources.workable.com /stories-and-insights/employee-burnout.

10 Business.com. 2021. "Why you need to worry about employee burnout." *Business.com.* Accessed December 14, 2021. https://www .business.com/articles/why-you-need-to-worry-about-burnout.

11 Schaufeli, W B, M Salanova, V Gonzalez-Roma, and A B Bakker. 2002. "The measurement of engagement and burnout: A two-sample factor analytic approach." *Journal of Happiness Studies* 71–92.

12 Harter, Jim. 2021. "US employee engagement holds steady in first half of 2021." *Gallup Workplace.* July 29. Accessed December 14, 2021. https://www.gallup.com/workplace/352949/employee -engagement-holds-steady-first-half-2021.aspx.

13 Gallup. 2021. "What is employee engagement and how do you improve it?" *Gallup Workplace.* Accessed December 14, 2021. https:// www.gallup.com/workplace/285674/improve-employee-engagement -workplace.aspx.

14 Spencer, Jean. 2020. "Research: Employee retention a bigger problem than hiring for small business." *Workest by Zenefits.* July 8. Accessed December 14, 2021. https://www.zenefits.com/workest /employee-turnover-infographic.

15 Smarp. 2021. "8 employee engagement statistics you need to know." *Smarp blog.* January 4. Accessed December 14, 2021. https://blog .smarp.com/employee-engagement-8-statistics-you-need-to-know.

16 Harter 2021.

17 Czeisler, Mark E, Rashon I Lane, Emiko Petrosky, Joshua F Wiley, Aleta Christensen, Rashid Njai, Matthew D Weaver, et al. 2020. "Mental health, substance use, and suicidal ideation during the COVID-19 pandemic." *MMWR*, August 14: 1049–1057.

18 Robinson, Bryan. 2020. "Grappling with the rise of work-related suicide during the pandemic: How to support yourself and fellow co-workers." *Forbes.com.* September 5. Accessed December 14, 2021. https://www.forbes.com/sites/bryanrobinson/2020/09/05/grappling -with-the-rise-of-work-related-suicide-during-the-pandemic-how-to -support-yourself-and-fellow-co-workers/?sh=28def90748d2.

19 Germain, Marie-Line. 2014. "Work-related suicide: An analysis of US government reports and recommendations for human resources." *Employee Relations* 36 (2): 148–164.

20 Grossmeier, J and Nikki Hudsmith. 2015. "Exploring the value proposition for workforce health: Business leader attitudes about the role of health as a driver of productivity and performance. *American Journal of Health Promotion* 29 (6): TAHP2–TAHP5.

21 LifeWorks. 2019. "Employee well-being is critical to business success, say CEOs." Accessed March 11, 2022. https://wellbeing.lifeworks .com/ca/blog/employee-well-being-is-critical-to-business-success -say-ceos.

22 Future Workplace. 2021. "Future Workplace: 2021 HR Sentiment Survey." Accessed March 11, 2022. https://futureworkplace.com /ebooks/2021-hr-sentiment-survey.

23 Linnan, L, L Cluff, and J Lang. 2019. "Results of the workplace health in America survey." *American Journal of Health Promotion* 33 (5): 652–665.

24 Moss, J. 2021. *The Burnout Epidemic.* Boston: Harvard Business Review Press.

25 Golden, J, R L Piedmont, J W Ciarrocchi, T Rodgerson. 2004. "Spirituality and burnout: An incremental validity study." *Journal of Psychology and Theology* 32 (2): 115–125.

26 Grossmeier, J, P H Castle, J S Pitts, C Saringer, K R Jenkins, M T Imboden, D J Mangen, S S Johnson, S P Noeldner, and S T Mason. 2020. "Workplace well-being factors that predict employee participation, health and medical cost impact, and perceived support." *American Journal of Health Promotion* 34 (4): 349–358. Goetzel, R Z, R M Henke, M Tabrizi, K R Pelletier, R Loeppke, D W Ballard, J Grossmeier, et al. 2014. "Do workplace health promotion (wellness) programs work?" *Journal of Occupational and Environmental Medicine* 56 (9): 927–934.

27 Terry P. 2016. "The Well-being Issue." *American Journal of Health Promotion* 30 (3): TAHP1.

28 Allen, Tim. 2021. "The pandemic is changing employee benefits." *Harvard Business Review Human Resource Management*. April 7. Accessed December 14, 2021. https://hbr.org/2021/04/the-pandemic -is-changing-employee-benefits.

29 Hettler, Bill. 1976. "The six dimensions of wellness model." *National Wellness Institute*. Accessed December 14, 2021. https:// nationalwellness.org/resources/six-dimensions-of-wellness.

30 Chapman, Larry. 1986. "Spiritual health: A component missing from health promotion." *American Journal of Health Promotion* 1 (1): 38–41.

31 Chapman, L. 2019. "Spiritual health revisited." *American Journal of Health Promotion* 33 (7): 1081–1093.

32 Ibid.

33 Neal, J. 2018. "Overview of workplace spirituality research." In *Palgrave Handbook of Workplace Spirituality and Fulfillment*, by S Dhiman, G E Roberts and J Crossman, 3–58. Cham: Palgrave Macmillan.

34 Galen, M, and K West. 1995. "Companies hit the road less travelled: Can spirituality enlighten the bottom line?" *Business Week*. June 5: 82–85.

35 Biberman, J. 2017. "Research and teaching on spirituality and spiritual leadership in management." *Graziadio Business Review* 20 (3).

36 Galen and West. 1995. "Companies hit the road less travelled: Can spirituality enlighten the bottom line?"

37 Cullen, J G. 2016. "Nursing management, religion, and spirituality: A bibliometric review, a research agenda, and implications for practice." *Journal of Nursing Management* 24 (3): 291–299.

38   Terry, Paul and Karen Moseley. 2019. "Thriving organizations: Achieving well-being through collaboration. HERO Forum19 Conference Proceedings. Health Enhancement Research Organization." Accessed March 15, 2022. https://hero-health.org /wp-content/uploads/2019/10/HERO-FORUM-PRO-112519.pdf; Nathan, Andrea, Karen Villanueva, and Julianna Rozek 2018. "The role of the built environment on health across the life course: A call for collaborACTION." *American Journal of Health Promotion* 32 (6): 1460–1468; Sorensen, Glorian, et al. 2013. "Integration of health protection and health promotion: Rationale, indicators, and metrics." *Journal of Occupational and Environmental Medicine* 55 (12 0): S12–S18.

39   Putnam, Laura. 2015. *Workplace Wellness That Works*. Hoboken: John Wiley & Sons.

40   Peele, Brandon. 2022. *Purpose Work Nation*. United States: Brandon Peele.

41   Schrage, Michael. 1990. *Shared Minds: The New Technologies of Collaboration*. New York: Random House.

42   Neal, J A. 2018. "Annotated list of workplace spirituality organizations." *Management, Spirituality & Religion – Workplace Spirituality*. Accessed December 14, 2021. https://msr.aom.org /resources/workplacespirituality.

43   Gill, Roger. 2022. "Introduction to Spirituality." In *Workplace Spirituality: Making a Difference*, by Yochanan Altman, Judi Neal, and Wolfgang Mayrhofer (Eds.), 21–73. Boston: Walter de Gruyter GmbH.

44   Fetzer Institute. 2020. "Study of Spirituality in the United States." Accessed March 15, 2022. https://fetzer.org/resources/what-does -spirituality-mean-us.

45   McClintock, C H, E Lau, and Lisa Miller. (2016). "Pheonotypic Dimensions of Spirituality: Implications for Mental Health in China, India, and the United States." *Frontiers in Psychology* 7 (1600) 1-16.

46   Miller, Lisa. 2021. *The Awakened Brain: The New Science of Spirituality and Our Quest for an Inspired Life*. New York: Random House.

47   Gomez, R, and J W Fisher. 2003. "Domains of spiritual well-being and development and validation of the Spiritual Well-being Questionnaire. *Personality and Individual Differences.* 35: 1975–1991.

48   Neal, J A. 2018.

49   Joly, Hubert, and Caroline Lambert. 2021. *The Heart of Business: Leadership Principles for the Next Era of Capitalism.* Boston: Harvard Business Review Press.

50   Metin, U B, Toon W Taris, Maria C W Peeters, and Ilona van Beek. 2016. "Authenticity at work – a job-demands resources perspective." *Journal of Managerial Psychology* 31 (2): 483–499.

51   Christakis, N A, and J H Fowler. 2011. *Connected: The Surprising Power of Our Social Networks and How They Shape Our Lives.* New York: Little, Brown and Company.

52   Orfanos, C E. 2007. "From Hippocrates to modern medicine." *Journal of the European Academy of Dermatology and Venereology* 21 (6): 852–858.

53   Harrington, S. 2016. "America's Healthiest Campus: The OSU well-being strategy model." *American Journal of Health Promotion* (Sage) 30 (3): TAHP2–TAHP3.

54   Centers for Disease Control and Prevention (CDC). 2018. *Well-being concepts.* Accessed December 14, 2021. https://www.cdc.gov/hrqol /wellbeing.htm#three.

55   HHS. 2018. "Issue Briefs to Inform Development and Implementation of Healthy People 2030." *Secretary's Advisory Committee for Healthy People 2030.* November. Accessed December 14, 2021. https://www.healthypeople.gov/sites/default/files /HP2030_Committee-Combined-Issue%20Briefs_2019-508c.pdf.

56   Johnson & Johnson Services, Inc. 2021. *Human Performance Institute.* Accessed November 2021. https://www.humanperformance institute.com.

57   Peele Brandon. n.d. "Purpose 101." Accessed February 27, 2022. http://brandonpeele.weebly.com/purpose-101.html.

58   Huta, Veronika. 2015. "The complementary roles of eudaimonia and hedonia and how they can be pursued in practice." In *Positive Psychology in Practice: Promoting Human Flourishing in Work, Health, Education, and Everyday Life*, by Stephen Joseph, 159–182. Hoboken, NJ: John Wiley & Sons, Inc; Strecher, Victor J. 2016. *Life on Purpose: How Living for What Matters Most Changes Everything.* New York: HarperCollins.

59   Ibid.

60   Newman, Kira M. 2020. *How purpose changes across your lifetime.* Greater Good Science Center. July 14. Accessed November 2021. https://greatergood.berkeley.edu/article/item/how_purpose _changes_across_your_lifetime.

61   Strecher, Victor J. 2016.

62   Burson, A, J Crocker, and D Mischkowski. 2012. "Two types of value-affirmation: implications for self-control following social exclusion." *Social Psychological and Personality Science* 3 (4): 510–516.

63   Yemiscigil, Ayse, and Ivo Vlaev. 2021. "The bidirectional relationship between sense of purpose in life and physical activity: a longitudinal study." *Journal of Behavioral Medicine* (Springer) 44: 715–725.

64   Strecher, Victor J. 2016.

65   Kim, Eric S, Koichiro Shiba, Julia K Boehm, and Laura D Kubzansky. 2020. "Sense of purpose in life and five health behaviors in older adults." *Preventive Medicine* 106172–106178.

66   Kim, Eric S, Victor J Strecher, and Carol D Ryff. 2014. "Purpose in life and use of preventive health care services." *Proceedings of the National Academy of Sciences* 111 (46) 16331–16336.

67   Gauen, Claire. 2021. "The Science of Living with Purpose." *The Ampersand.* September 2. Accessed November 15, 2021. https://artsci.wustl.edu/ampersand/science-living-purpose.

68   Dahl, Cortland. 2021. "How to create a sense of purpose according to science." *Elemental.* March 31. Accessed November 15, 2021. https://elemental.medium.com/how-to-create-a-sense-of-purpose -according-to-science-17ba921e1e6e.

69   Arnold, K A, N Turner, J Barling, E K Kelloway, and M C McKee. 2007. "Transformational leadership and psychological well-being: the mediating role of meaningful work." *Journal of Occupational Health Psychology* (APA) 12 (3): 193–203; Schaefer, Stacey M, Jennifer Morozink Boylan, Carien M van Reekum, Regina C Lapate, Catherine J Norris, Carol D Ryff, and Richard J Davidson. 2013. "Purpose in life predicts better emotional recovery from negative stimuli." *PLoS One* (PLoS One) 8 (11): e80329.

70   Kim, Eric S, Ying Chen, Julie S. Nakamara, Carol D. Ryff, and Tyler J. VanderWeele. 2022. "The sense of purpose in life and subsequent physical, behavioral, and psychosocial health: An outcome-wide approach." *American Journal of Health Promotion* 36 (1): 137–147.

71   Sisodia, R, D B Wolfe, and J Sheth. 2014. *Firms of Endearment.* Upper Saddle River, NJ: Prentice Hall.

72   Johnson, Sara S. 2019. "The potential and promise of purpose-driven organizations." *American Journal of Health Promotion* (Sage) 33 (6): 958–973; Hurst, Aaron, Brandon Peele, Tim Kelley, and Ach Mercurio. "The Science of Purpose." Licensed under Creative Commons Attribution 4.0 International License. Accessed February 27, 2022. http://scienceofpurpose.org.

73   Quinn, Robert and Anjan V. Thakor. 2019. *The Economics of Higher Purpose.* Oakland: Berrett-Koehler Publishers, Inc.

74   Emmett, Jonathan, Gunnar Schrah, Matt Schrimper, and Alexandra Wood. 2020. "COVID-19 and the employee experience: How leaders can seize the moment." *McKinsey & Company.* June. Accessed November 15, 2021. https://www.mckinsey.com/~/media/McKinsey /Business%20Functions/Organization/Our%20Insights/COVID%20 19%20and%20the%20employee%20experience%20How%20 leaders%20can%20seize%20the%20moment/COVID-19-and-t he-employee-experience-How-leaders-can-seize-the-moment.pdf; Fairlie, Paul. 2011. "Meaningful work, employee engagement, and other key employee outcomes: Implications for Human Resource development." *Advances in Developing Human Resources* (Sage) 13 (4): 508–525.

75   PWC. 2016. "Putting Purpose to Work: A study of purpose in the workplace." *PWC.* June. Accessed November 15, 2021. https://www .pwc.com/us/en/about-us/corporate-responsibility/assets/pwc-putting -purpose-to-work-purpose-survey-report.pdf.

76 Reece, Andrew, Gabriella Kellerman, and Alexi Robichaus. 2018. "Meaning and Purpose at Work." Accessed February 27, 2022. https://grow.betterup.com/resources/meaning-and-purpose-report?hsLang=en.

77 Victor J Strecher, personal communication.

78 Edelman. 2021. Edelman Trust Barometer 2021. Accessed March 15, 2022. https://www.edelman.com/sites/g/files/aatuss191/files/2021-03/2021%20Edelman%20Trust%20Barometer.pdf.

79 Achor, Shawn, Gabriella Rosen Kellerman, Andrew Reece, and Alexi Robichaux. 2018. "America's Loneliest Workers, According to Research." *Harvard Business Review.* March 19. Accessed February 27, 2022. https://hbsp.harvard.edu/product/H0483R-PDF-ENG.

80 Emmett, et al. 2020.

81 Peele. 2022.

82 Burrow, Anthony L, Maclen Stanley, Rachel Sumner, and Patrick L. Hill. 2014. "Purpose in Life as a Resource for Increasing Comfort with Ethnic Diversity." *Personality and Social Psychology Bulletin* 40 (11): 1507–1516.

83 Imperative. n.d. "Why Imperative?" Accessed March 15, 2022. https://www.imperative.com/why-imperative-companies; Johnson & Johnson Services, Inc. 2021. *Human Performance Institute.* Accessed November 2021. https://www.humanperformanceinstitute.com.

84 Unity Lab. 2022. "Our Story." Accessed March 15, 2022. https://www.unitylab.co.

85 Johnson & Johnson Services, Inc. 2021.

86 Herway, Jake. 2021. "Just How Purpose-Driven Is Your Organization?" *Gallup Workplace.* October 22. Accessed November 15, 2021. https://www.gallup.com/workplace/356093/purpose-driven-organizational-culture.aspx.

87 Emmett, et al. 2020.

88 Willroth, E C, Daniel K Mroczek, and Patrick L Hill. 2021. "Maintaining sense of purpose in midlife predicts better physical health." *Journal of Psychosomatic Research* 145: 110485.

89 Newman. 2020.

90 Johnson. 2019.

91 Rey Carlos, Miquel Bastons, and Phil Sotok. 2019. *Purpose-Driven Organizations: Management Ideas for a Better World.* London: Palgrave Macmillan.

92 Best Buy. 2021. "Best Buy Awards & Recognition." Accessed March 15, 2022. https://corporate.bestbuy.com/awards-and-recognition.

93 Best Buy. 2021. "Fiscal 2021 Annual Report." Accessed February 27, 2022. http://s2.q4cdn.com/785564492/files/doc_financials/2021/ar/Best-Buy_Annual-Report_FY21.pdf.

94 Joly, Hubert. 2022. *The Heart of Business.* Boston: Harvard Business Review Press.

95 Kumanu, Inc. n.d. *Creating a purpose-fueled culture.* Ann Arbor, MI. www.kumanu.com.

96 Loehr, Jim. 2021. *Leading with Character: 10 Minutes a Day to a Brilliant Legacy.* Hoboken, NJ: John Wiley & Sons.

97 Clance, Pauline R, and Suzanne A Imes. 1978. "The imposter phenomenon in high achieving women: Dynamics and therapeutic intervention." *Psychotherapy: Theory, Research & Practice* 15 (3): 241–247.

98 Loehr. 2021.

99 Cigna. 2020. "Loneliness in the Workplace." *Cigna newsroom.* January. Accessed November 19, 2021. https://www.cigna.com/static/www-cigna-com/docs/about-us/newsroom/studies-and-reports/combatting-loneliness/cigna-2020-loneliness-report.pdf.

100 Saporito, Thomas J. 2012. "It's time to acknowledge CEO loneliness." *Harvard Business Review*, February 15.

101 Brown, Brené. 2012. *Daring Greatly: How the Courage to Be Vulnerable Transforms the Way We Live, Love, Parent, and Lead.* New York: Penguin Random House.

102 O' Donohue, John. 1999. *Celtic Reflections on our Yearning to Belong.* New York: HarperCollins Publishers.

103 Holt-Lunstad, Julianne. 2018. "Fostering social connection in the workplace." *American Journal of Health Promotion* (Sage) 32 (5): 1304–1318.

104 Fisher, Jen, and Anh Phillips. 2021. *Work Better Together: How to Cultivate Strong Relationships to Maximize Well-being and Boost Bottom Lines.* New York: McGraw Hill.

105 Uchino, Bert N. 2006. "Social support and health: A review of physiological processes potentially underlying links to disease outcomes." *Journal of Behavioral Medicine* (Springer) 29: 377–387.

106 Holt-Lunstad, Julianne, and Bert N Uchino. 2015. *Social support and health*. Vol. 5, in *Health Behavior Theory, Research, and Practice*, by Karen Glanz, Barbara K Rimer and K Viswanath. San Francisco: John Wiley & Sons, Inc.

107 Boss, Lisa, Duck-Hee Kang, and Sandy Branson. 2015. "Loneliness and cognitive function in the older adult: A systematic review." *International Psychogeriatrics* (Cambridge University Press) 27 (4): 541–553; Calmasini C, Swinnerton KN, et al. 2022. "Association of Social Integration with Cognitive Status in a Multi-Ethnic Cohort: Results from the Kaiser Healthy Aging and Diverse Life Experiences Study." *Journal of Geriatric Psychiatry and Neurology* doi:10.1177/08919887211070259.

108 Werner-Seidler, Aliza, Mohammad H Afzali, Cath Chapman, Matthew Sunderland, and Tim Slade. 2017. "The relationship between social support networks and depression in the 2007 National Survey of Mental Health and Well-being." *Social Psychiatry and Psychiatric Epidemiology* (Springer) 52: 1463–1473.

109 Clair, Ruta, Maya Gordon, Matthew Kroon, and Carolyn Reilly. 2021. "The effects of social isolation on well-being and life satisfaction during the pandemic." *Humanities and Social Sciences Communications* 8 (28).

110 Pfitzinger, Julie. 2020. "Dr. Jeremy Noble Believes It's Okay to Say 'I'm Lonely.'" *Next Avenue.* Accessed March 11, 2022. https://www.nextavenue.org/dr-jeremy-nobel-believes-its-okay-to-say-im-lonely.

111 Hawkley, Louise C, and John P Capitanio. 2015. "Perceived social isolation, evolutionary fitness and health outcomes: A lifespan approach." *Philosophical Transactions* B 370: 20140114. http://dx.doi.org/10.1098/rstb.2014.0114.

112 Spithoven, Annette W M, Patricia Bijttebier, and Luc Goossens. 2017. "It is all in their mind: A review on information processing bias in lonely individuals." *Clincal Psychology Review*, December: 97–114.

113 Saporito. 2012.

114 Holt-Lunstad, Julianne. 2018. "Fostering social connection in the workplace." *American Journal of Health Promotion* (Sage) 32 (5): 1304–1318.

115 Johnson, Sara S. 2019.

116 Murthy, Vivek. 2017. "Work and the loneliness epidemic: Reducing isolation at work is good for business." *Harvard Business Review*, September 26.

117 Barsade, Sigal G, and Olivia A O'Neill. 2014. "What's love got to do with it? A longitudinal study of the culture of companionate love and employee and client outcomes in a long-term care setting." *Administrative Science Quarterly* 59 (4): 551–598.

118 Carr, Evan W, Andrew Reece, Gabriella Rosen Kellerman, and Alexi Robichaux. 2019. "The value of belonging at work." *Harvard Business Review*, December 16. Accessed February 22, 2022. https://hbr.org/2019/12/the-value-of-belonging-at-work.

119 Cameron, Kim S, and B Winn. 2012. "Virtuousness in organizations." In *Oxford Handbook of Positive Organizational Scholarship*, by Kim S Cameron and G M Spreitzer. New York: Oxford University Press.

120 Ibid.

121 Emmett, et al. 2020.

122 Holt-Lunstad. 2018.

123 Fisher and Phillips. 2021.

124 Peele. 2022.

125 Worthington, E L, and N G Wade. 1999. "The psychology of unforgiveness and implications for clinical practice." *Journal of Social and Clinical Psychology* 18 (4): 385–418.

126 Toussaint, Loren, Frederic Luskin, Rick Aberman, and Arthur DeLorenzo. 2019. "Is forgiveness one of the secrets to success? Considering the costs of workplace disharmony and the benefits of teaching employees to forgive." *American Journal of Health Promotion* 33 (7): 1090–1093.

127 Authentic Revolution. 2022. "What is Authentic Relating?" Accessed February 22, 2022. https://www.authrev.org/what-is-authentic-relating.

128 Vogl, Charles H. 2016. *The Art of Community: Seven Principles of Belonging.* Oakland, CA: Berrett-Koehler Publishers, Inc.

129 Lisa Olson, personal communication.

130 Michelle Railton, personal communication.

131 Anwar, Mohammad F, Frank E Danna, Jeffrey F Ma, and Christopher J Pitre. 2021. *Love as a Business Strategy.* Lioncress Publishing.

132 Softway Solutions LLP. 2021. *Seneca Leaders.* Accessed November 23, 2021. https://www.loveasabusinessstrategy.com/seneca-laabs.

133 Maslow, Abraham H. 1971. *The Farther Reaches of Human Nature.* New York: Arkana/Penguin Books.

134 Haugan, Gorill and Siw Tone Innstrand. 2012. "The effect of self-transcendence on depression in cognitively intact nursing home patients." *International Scholarly Research Network* doi:10.5402/2012/301325.

135 Ibid.

136 Dethmer Jim, Diana Chapman, and Kaley Warner Klemp. 2014. *The 15 Commitments of Conscious Leadership: A New Paradigm for Sustainable Success.* Conscious Leadership Group and Kaley Warner Klemp.

137 Renee Moorefield, personal communication.

138 Yaden, David Bryce, Jonathan Haidt, Ralph W Hood, David R Vago, and Andrew B Newberg. 2017. "The varieties of self-transcendent experience." *Review of General Psychology* 21: 143–160.

139 Allen, Summer. 2018. *The Science of Awe.* White paper, UC Berkeley, Berkeley: Greater Good Science Center, 45; Ter Kuile, Casper. 2020. *The Power of Ritual: Turning Everyday Activities into Soulful Practices.* New York: HarperCollins Publishers.

140 Wong, P T P. 2016. Meaning-seeking, self-transcendence, and well-being. In Batthyany (Ed.), *Logotherapy and existential analysis: Proceedings of the Viktor Frankl Institute* Vol. 1, 311–322. Cham, CH: Springer.

141 Kitson, Alexandra, Alice Chirico, Andrea Gaggioli, and Bernhard E Riecke. 2020. "A review on research and evaluation methods for investigating self-transcendence." *Frontiers in Psychology* 11 (547687); Van Cappellen, Patty, and Bernard Rime. 2014. "Positive emotions and self-transcendence." In *Religion, Personality, and Social Behavior,* by V. Saroglou, 123–145. New York: Psychology Press.

142 Ter Kuile. 2020.

143 Hanh, Thich Nhat. 2006. *The Energy of Prayer: How to Deepen Your Spiritual Practice.* Berkeley: Parallax Press.

144 Wong. 2016.

145 Keltner, D J, and J Haidt. 2003. "Approaching awe, a moral, spiritual, and aesthetic emotion." *Cognition and Emotion* 17 (2): 297–314.

146 Ekman, P, and D Cordaro. 2011. "What is meant by calling emotions basic." *Emotion Review* 3 (4): 364–370.

147 Kitson, et al. 2020.

148 Kaufman, Scott Barry. 2021. *Transcend: The New Science of Self-Actualization.* New York: Penguin Random House LLC; Yaden, et al. 2017. Kitson, et al. 2020.

149 Messerly, John G. 2017. *Summary of Maslow on Self-Transcendence.* February 4. Accessed November 29, 2021. https://archive.ieet.org /articles/Messerly20170204.html.

150 Yaden, et al. 2017.

151 Kitson, et al. 2020.

152 Wong. 2016.

153 Haugan and Innstrand. 2012.

154 Yaden, et al. 2017.

155 Stellar, J E, N John-Henderson, C L Anderson, A M Gordon, G D McNeil, and D J Keltner. 2015. "Positive affect and markers of inflammation: discrete positive emotions predict lower levels of inflammatory cytokines." *Emotion* 15 (2): 129–133.

156 Allen. 2018.

157 Yaden, et al. 2017.

158 Chin, Brian. J Slutsky, J Raye, J David Creswell. 2019. "Mindfulness training reduces stress at work: A randomized controlled trial." *Mindfulness* 10 (4): 627-638.

159 Irving, J A, P L Dobkin, J Park. 2009. "Cultivating mindfulness in health care professionals: A review of empirical studies of mindfulness-based stress reduction." *Complementary Therapy Clinical Practice* 15 (2): 61-66.

160 Rogers, Kristen. 2020. "The psychological benefits of prayer: What science says about the mind-soul connection." *CNN Health: Life, But Better.* June 17. Accessed November 29, 2021. https://www.cnn.com/2020/06/17/health/benefits-of-prayer-wellness/index.html.

161 Epel, Elissa and Elizabeth Blackburn. 2017. *The Telomere Effect.* New York: Grand Central Publishing.

162 Hoge, E A, M M Chen, E Orr, C A Metcalf, L E Fischer, M H Pollack, I De Vivo, N M Simon. 2013. "Loving-kindness meditation practice associated with longer telomeres in women." *Brain, Behavior, and Immunity* 32: 159–163; Le Nguyen, K D, J Lin, S B Algoe, M M Brantley, S L Kim, J Brantley, S Salzberg, B L Fredrickson. 2019. "Loving-kindness meditation slows biological aging in novices: Evidence from a 12-week randomized controlled trial." *Psychoneuroendocrinology* 108: 20–27.

163 Holzel, B K, J Carmody, M Vangel, C Congleton, S M Yerramsetti, T Gard, S W Lazar. 2011. "Mindfulness practice leads to increases in regional brain gray matter density." *Psychiatry Research: Neuroimaging.* 191 (1): 36-43.

164 Greiser, Christian, Jan-Philipp Martini, and Nicole Meissner. 2018. "Unleashing the power of mindfulness in corporations." Boston Consulting Group. Accessed March 21, 2022. https://www.bcg.com/en-us/publications/2018/unleashing-power-of-mindfulness-in-corporations.

165 Yaden, et al. 2017.

166 Dahl, C J, C D Wilson-Mendenhall, R J Davidson. 2020. "The plasticity of well-being: A training-based framework for the cultivation of human flourishing." *Proceedings of the National Academy of Sciences* 117 (51): 32197–32206; Good, D J, C Lyddy, T M Glomb, J E Bono, K W Brown, M K Duffy, R A Baer, J A Brewer, S W Lazar. 2015. "Contemplating mindfulness at work: An integrative review." *School of Management* 42 (1): 114–142; Chaskalson, M. 2011. *The Mindful Workplace; Developing Resilient Individuals and Resonant Organizations with MBSR.* Oxford, United Kingdom: Wiley.

167 Greiser, Martini, and Meissner. 2018.

168 Goleman, Daniel, and Richard J Davidson. 2017. *Altered Traits: Science Reveals How Meditation Changes Your Mind, Brain, and Body.* New York: Avery.

169 Gray, Jeremy R, John Dovidio, and John F Dovidio. 2014. "The nondiscriminating heart: Lovingkindness meditation training decreases implicit intergroup bias." *Journal of Experimental Psychology: General* 143 (3): 1306–1313; Stell, Alexander J, and T Farsides. 2016. "Brief loving-kindness meditation reduces racial bias, mediated by other-regarding emotions." *Motivation and Emotion* (Springer) 40: 140–147.

170 Allen. 2018; Piff, Paul K, P Dietze, M Feinberg, D M Stancato, and D Keltner. 2015. "Awe, the small self, and prosocial behavior." *Journal of Personality and Social Psychology* 108 (6): 883–899; Kitson, et al. 2020; Kitson, Alexandra, Alice Chirico, Andrea Gaggioli, and Bernhard E Riecke. 2020. "A review on research and evaluation methods for investigating self-transcendence." *Frontiers in Psychology* 11 (547687); Van Cappellen, Patty, and Bernard Rime. 2014. "Positive emotions and self-transcendence." In *Religion, Personality, and Social Behavior*, by V Saroglou, 123–145. New York: Psychology Press.

171 Wisdom Works. 2021. "Effectively Leading Through Paradox: A Pivotal Role for Wellbeing." Be Well Lead Well® Research Insights. Accessed February 28, 2022. https://www.bewellleadwell.com /wp-content/uploads/2021/06/BeWellLeadWell-Research-Insights -Paradoxical-Leadership-Report-2021.pdf.

172 Renee Moorefield, personal communication.

173 Palmer, Beth, Mary T Quinn Griffin, Pamela Reed, and Joyce J Fitzpatrick. 2010. "Self-transcendence and work engagement in acute care staff registered nurses." *Critical Care Nursing Quarterly* 33 (2): 138–147.

174 Good, et al. 2015; Olejniczak L. 2021. "Why Google, Target, and General Mills Are Investing in Mindfulness." Small Business Association of Michigan. January 8. Accessed February 27, 2022. https://www.sbam.org/why-google-target-and-general-mills-are -investing-in-mindfulness/; Greiser, Martini, and Meissner 2018.

175 Kachan Diana, Henry Olano, Stacey L. Tannenbaum, Debra W. Annane, Ashwin Mehta, Kristopher L. Arheart et al. 2017. "Prevalence of mindfulness practices in the US Workforce: National Health Interview Survey." *Preventing Chronic Disease* 14 (1):160034 10.5888/pcd14.160034.

176 Appelbaum, Steven H and Adam Marchionni. 2008. "The multitasking paradox: Perceptions, problems and strategies." *Management Decision* 46 (9): 1313–1325.

177 Ibid.

178 Fuller, Ryan, Nina Shikaloff, Renee Cullinan, and Shani Harmon. 2018. "If You Multitask During Meetings, Your Team Will, Too." *Harvard Business Review*. January 25. Accessed February 26, 2022. https://hbr.org/2018/01/if-you-multitask-during-meetings -your-team-will-too.

179 Williams, Ray. 2014. "Why reflection and doing nothing are critical for productivity." *Financial Post*. August 15, 2014. Accessed March 28, 2022. https://financialpost.com/executive/leadership/why -reflection-and-doing-nothing-are-critical-for-productivity.

180 Yaden, et al. 2017.

181 Neal, Judi. 2018. "Overview of workplace spirituality research." In *The Palgrave Handbook of Workplace Spirituality and Fulfillment*, by S Dhiman, 3–57. Switzerland: Palgrave Macmillan.

182 Ter Kuile. 2020.

183 Ozenc, Kursat, and Margaret Hagan. 2019. *Rituals for Work.* Hoboken: John Wiley & Sons.

184 Ouimet, J Robert. 2014. "In Search of an Organization that Shines." *Notre Projet*. Accessed November 30, 2021. http://www.notreprojet.org/?page_id=3940&lang=en.

185 Ibid.

186 Ibid.

187 Fetzer Institute. 2018. "Our Culture." Accessed March 14, 2022. https://fetzer.org/community/culture.

188 Ibid.

189 Fetzer Institute. 2020. "Co-Creating Our Story." Kalamazoo: Fetzer Institute. Accessed March 14, 2022. https://fetzer.org/resources/co-creating-our-story-hybrid-participatory-case-approach-evaluating-and-accelerating.

190 Ibid.

191 Linnan, Cluff, and Lang. 2019.

192 Terry. 2019.

193 World Health Organization. 1986. "The 1st International Conference on Health Promotion, Ottawa, 1986." *Health Promotion*. Accessed December 1, 2021. https://www.who.int/teams/health-promotion/enhanced-wellbeing/first-global-conference.

194 Sallis, James F, Neville Owen, and Edwin B Fisher. 2008. "Ecological models of health behavior." In *Health Behavior and Health Education: Theory, Research, and Practice*, by Karen Glanz, Barbara K Rimer and K Viswanath, 465–486. San Francisco: Jossey-Bass.

195 Neal, Judi. 2018. "Overview of workplace spirituality research." In *The Palgrave Handbook of Workplace Spirituality and Fulfillment*, by Satinder Dhiman, Gary E Roberts, and Joanna Crossman. Palgrave Macmillan.

196 Kinjerski, V. 2013. "The spirit at work scale: Developing and validating a measure of individual spirituality at work." In *Handbook of Faith and Spirituality in the Workplace*, by Judi Neal, 383–402. New York: Springer.

197 Weziak-Bialowolska, Dorota, Piotr Bialowolski, Matthew T Lee, Ying Chen, Tyler J VanderWeele, and Eileen McNeely. 2021. "Psychometric properties of flourishing scales from a comprehensive well-being assessment." *Frontiers in Psychology* 12 (652209).

198 Soler, R E, K D Leeks, S Razi, D P Hopkins, M Griffith, A Aten, S K Chattopadhyay, et al. 2010. "A systematic review of selected interventions for worksite health promotion: the assessment of health risks with feedback." *American Journal of Preventive Medicine* 38 (2 Supplement): S237–S262.

199 del Carmen Perez-Fuentes, Maria, Maria del Mar Molero Jurado, Isabel Mercader Rubio, Jose Gabriel Soriano Sanchez, and Jose Jesus Gazquez Linares. 2020. "Mindfulness for preventing psychosocial risks in the workplace: A systematic review and meta-analysis." *Applied Sciences* 10 (5): 1851; Bartlett, L, A Martin, A Neil, K Memish, P Otahal, Kilpatrick M, and K Sanderson. 2019. "A systematic review and meta-analysis of workplace mindfulness training randomized controlled trials." *Journal of Occupational Health Psychology* 24 (1): 108–126; Lomas, Tim, Juan Carlos Medina, Itai Ivtzan, Silke Rupprecht, and Francisco Jose Eiroa-Orosa. 2019. "Mindfulness-based interventions in the workplace: An inclusive systematic review and meta-analysis of their impact upon wellbeing." *Journal of Positive Psychology* 14 (5): 625–640.

200 Greater Good Science Center. 2021. "Keys to well-being." Accessed December 15, 2021. https://greatergood.berkeley.edu/key.

201 Trandel, Darlene. 2018. "Advancing the practice of professional health and wellness coaching." In *Professional Coaching: Principles and Practice*, by Susan English, Janice Manzi Sabatine and Philip Brownell, 369–384. New York: Springer.

202 Hall, Chad. 2018. "Coaching and spirituality: A mutually resourceful relationship." In *Professional Coaching: Principles and Practice*, by Susan English, Janice Manzi Sabatine and Philip Brownell, 399–410. New York: Springer.

203 Seales, Chad E. 2012. "Corporate chaplaincy and the American workplace." *Religion Compass* 6 (3): 195–203.

204 Miller, David W, Faith Wambura Ngunjiri, and James D LoRusso. 2017. "Human resources perceptions of corporate chaplains: enhancing positive organizational culture." *Journal of Management, Spirituality & Religion* 14 (3): 196–215.

205 Miller, David W, Faith Wambura Ngunjiri, and James D LoRusso. 2018. "'The suits care about us': Employee perceptions of workplace chaplains." *Journal of Management, Spirituality & Religion* 15 (5): 377–397.

206 Grossmeier, Jessica, and Emily Wolfe. 2017. "University of Michigan case study: MHealthy Creating a culture of health." *Health Enhancement Research Organization Committee Publications.* September. Accessed December 7, 2021. https://hero-health.org/resources/committee-publications.

207 Heermann, Barry. 1997. *Building Team Spirit: Activities for Inspiring and Energizing Teams.* New York: McGraw-Hill.

208 Harvey, Janet M. 2018. "What team coaching is and is not." In *Professional Coaching: Principles and Practice,* by Susan English, Janice Manzi Sabatine, and Philip Brownell, 384–398. New York: Springer.

209 Fisher and Phillips. 2021. *Work Better Together.*

210 Laszlo, Chris, and Judy Sorum Brown. 2014. *Flourishing Enterprise: The New Spirit of Business.* Stanford: Stanford University Press.

211 Quinn, Robert E and Anjan V Thakor. 2019. *The Economics of Higher Purpose: Eight Counterintuitive Steps for Creating a Purpose-Driven Organization.* Oakland: Berrett-Koehler Publishers, Inc.

212 Meacham Webb, Kathy, and Dan Krick. 2017. "A collaborative approach to defining a culture of health." *American Journal of Health Promotion* (Sage) 31 (6): 516–517.

213 Stokols, Daniel, Kenneth R Pelletier, and Jonathan E Fielding. 1996. "The ecology of work and health: Research and policy directions for promotion of employee health." *Health Education Quarterly* 23 (2): 137–158.

214 Tsao, Frederick Chavalit, and Chris Laszlo. 2019. *Quantum Leadership.* Stanford: Stanford Business Books.

215 Haanaes, Knut, Martin Reeves, Ingrid Von Streng Velken, Michael Audretsch, David Kiron, and Nina Kruschwitz. 2012. "Sustainability Nears a Tipping Point." *MIT Sloan Management Review.* January 23. Accessed December 8, 2021. https://sloanreview.mit.edu/projects/sustainability-nears-a-tipping-point.

216 Joly, Hubert. 2021.

217 Business Roundtable. 2019. "Business Roundtable Redefines the Purpose of a Corporation to Promote 'An Economy That Serves All Americans." August 19. Accessed February 23, 2022. https://www .businessroundtable.org/business-roundtable-redefines-the -purpose-of-a-corporation-to-promote-an-economy-that-serves -all-americans.

218 Laszlo and Sorum Brown. 2014.

219 Harvard T.H. Chan School of Public Health. n.d. *SHINE: About Us.* Accessed December 8, 2021. https://shine.sph.harvard.edu/about-us.

220 Harvard University. 2021. *The Human Flourishing Program.* Accessed December 8, 2021. https://hfh.fas.harvard.edu/projects.

221 Harvard University, 2021.

222 Health Enhancement Research Organization (HERO). 2020. "Healthy Workplaces, Healthy Communities: Why invest in community health?" Accessed April 11, 2022. http://get-hwhc.org /why-invest-in-community-health/the-healthy-connection-2.

223 Bipartisan Policy Center and de Beaumont. 2019. "Good Health is Good Business: The Value Proposition of Partnerships Between Businesses and Governmental Public Health Agencies to Improve Community Health." *Healthy Workplaces, Healthy Communities: Resources.* June. Accessed December 8, 2021. http://get-hwhc.org /resources/articles-videos-and-more.

224 Quinn and Thakor. 2019; Rey, Bastons and Sotok. 2019; Peele. 2022.

225 Quinn and Thakor. 2019.

226 Tsao and Laszlo. 2019.

227 Moorefield, Renee. 2019. "Effective leadership: What does spirituality have to do with it?" *American Journal of Health Promotion* (Sage) 33 (7): 1085–1087.

228 Johnson & Johnson.

229 Kenney, Caren. 2019. "Purpose and character: The ultimate differentiators of a legacy leader." *American Journal of Health Promotion* (Sage) 33 (7): 1087–1089.

230 Grossmeier, Jessica, and Mary Imboden. 2021. "HERO research identifies top ten scorecard practices." *2020 HERO Scorecard Progress Report.* January. Accessed December 8, 2021. https://hero-health.org /wp-content/uploads/2021/01/HERO-2020-Progress-Report.pdf.

231 Fry, L W. 2003. "Toward a theory of spiritual leadership." *Leadership Quarterly* 14 (6): 693–727.

232 Ibid.

233 Miller, William C, and Debra R Miller. 2008. "Spirituality: The emerging context for business leadership." *Global Dharma Center*. Accessed December 8, 2021. https://www.globaldharma.org/Files%20 -%20Adobe%20Acrobat/SBL/Spirituality.%20Emerging%20 Context%20for%20Bus.%20Ldrship%20UPDATED%20 Oct08.pdf.

234 Brower, Kirk J, Chantal M L R. Brazeau, Sharon C Kiely, et al. 2021. "The Evolving Role of the Chief Wellness Officer in the Management of Crises by Health Care Systems: Lessons from the Covid-19 Pandemic." *NEJM Catalyst* 2 (5); Biderman-Gross, F. 2020. "What's a Chief Purpose Officer and Why Should You Hire One?" *Forbes*, March 18. Accessed February 6, 2022. https://www.forbes.com/sites /forbesagencycouncil/2020/03/18/whats-a-chief-purpose-officer-and -why-should-you-hire-one/?sh=42a40f0a18e9; Shanafelt, Tait D, and Christine A Sinsky. 2020. "Establishing a Chief Wellness Officer Position. AMA STEPS Forward™. Accessed February 6, 2022. https:// edhub.ama-assn.org/steps-forward/module/2767739; Peele 2022; Brower, et al. 2021.

235 Shanafelt and Sinsky. 2020.

236 Terry, P E, J Grossmeier, D J Mangen, and S B Gingerich. 2013. "Analyzing best practices in employee health management: How age, gender, and program components relate to employee engagement and health outcomes." *Journal of Occupational and Environmental Medicine* 55 (4): 378–392; Grossmeier, J. 2013. "The influence of worksite and employee variables on employee engagement in telephonic health coaching programs." *American Journal of Health Promotion* 27 (3): e69; Terry P E, E L D Seaverson, J Grossmeier, and D R Anderson. 2008. "Association between nine quality components and superior worksite health management program results." *Journal of Occupational and Environmental Medicine* 50 (6): 633–641.

237 Grossmeier, J, R Fabius, J P Flynn, S P Noeldner, D Fabius, R Z Goetzel, and D R Anderson. 2016. "Linking workplace health promotion best practices and organizational financial performance: Tracking market performance of companies with highest scores on the HERO Scorecard." *Journal of Occupational and Environmental Medicine* 58 (1): 16–23; Grossmeier, J, D J Mangen, D R Anderson, S B Gingerich, R J Mitchell, M T Imboden, G D Kaplan, G M Gascon, S A Serxner, and T Bodak. 2020. "Influence of incentive design and organizational characteristics on wellness participation and health outcomes." *Journal of Occupational and Environmental Medicine* 62 (10): 874–882; Grossmeier, J, P H Castle, J S Pitts, C Saringer, K R Jenkins, M T Imboden, D J Mangen, S S Johnson, S P Noeldner, and S T Mason. 2020. "Workplace well-being factors that predict employee participation, health and medical cost impact, and perceived support." *American Journal of Health Promotion* 34 (4): 349–358.

238 Centers for Disease Control and Prevention. 2016. *Workplace Health Model.* May 13. Accessed December 2021. https://www.cdc.gov /workplacehealthpromotion/model/index.html.

239 Kinjerski, V. 2013.

240 Health Enhancement Research Organization. 2021. *HERO Scorecard.* Accessed December 8, 2021. https://hero-health.org/hero-scorecard.

241 Grossmeier, Castle, et al. 2020.

242 Grossmeier, J. 2020. "Updated employer tools identify practices associated with population health outcomes." *American Journal of Health Promotion* 34 (3): 316–317.

243 CDC 2015. *Workplace Health Model: Evaluation.* December 8. Accessed December 9, 2021. https://www.cdc.gov/workplace healthpromotion/model/evaluation/index.html.

244 Grossmeier, J. 2020. "A dashboard approach to demonstrating value." *American Journal of Health Promotion.* 34 (4): 447–465.

245 Grossmeier, Mangen, et al. 2020.

246 Karakas F. 2010. "Spirituality and performance in organizations: A literature review. *Journal of Business Ethics* 94: 89–106.

247 Ibid.

248 Houghton, J, C Neck, and S Krishnakumar. 2016. "The what, why, and how of spirituality in the workplace revisited: a 14-year update and extension." *Journal of Management, Spirituality & Religion* 13 (3): 177–205.

249 Ashmos, D, and D Duchon. 2000. "Spirituality at work: A conceptualization and measure." *Journal of Management Inquiry* 9 (2): 134–145.

250 Fornaciari, C J, and Dean K Lund. 2009. "Foundations, lessons, and insider tips for MSR research." *Journal of Management, Spirituality & Religion* 6 (4): 301–321.

251 Geigle, David. 2012. "Workplace spirituality empirical research: A literature review." *Business and Management Review* 2 (10): 14–27.

252 de Diego-Cordero, Rocio, Maria Paz Zurron Perez, Ana Magdalena Vargas-Martinez, Giancarlo Lucchetti, and Juan Vega-Escano. 2021. "The effectiveness of spiritual interventions in the workplace for work-related health outcomes: A systematic review and meta-analysis." *Journal of Nursing Management* (Wiley) 29 (6): 1703–1712.

253 Valle, Elisabetta Della, Stefano Palermi, Irene Aloe, Roberto Marcantonio, Rocco Spera, Stefania Montagnani, and Felice Sirico. 2020. "Effectiveness of workplace yoga interventions to reduce perceived stress in employees: A systematic review and meta-analysis." *Journal of Functional Morphology and Kinesiology* 5 (2): 33.

254 Geigle, D. 2012. "Workplace spirituality empirical research: A literature review." *Business Management Review* 2 (10): 14–27; Benefiel, Margaret, Louis W Fry, and David Geigle. 2014. "Spirituality and religion in the workplace: History, theory, and research." *Psychology of Religion and Spirituality* 6 (3): 175–187.

255 Koenig, Harold G. 2012. "Religion, spirituality, and health: The research and clinical implications." *International Scholarly Network* 29 (3): 19–26.

256 Godsil, Rachel D, and Brianna Goodale. 2013. "Telling Our Own Story: The Role of Narrative in Racial Healing." *America Healing*. June. Accessed December 13, 2021. http://perception.org /wp-content/uploads/2014/11/Telling-Our-Own-Story.pdf.

257 Grossmeier, Jessica, Carmine Gallo, Laura Putnam, Brian Passon, Shawn McCann, Jody Barto, Nancy Goldman, Elena Valentine, and Sara Johnson. 2019. "The Storytelling Issue." *American Journal of Health Promotion* (Sage) 33 (3): 1–16.

258 Lewis, M. 2017. *The Undoing Project.* New York: Norton & Company.

259 Vogl, Charles. 2020. *Storytelling for Leadership: Creating Authentic Connections.* Berkeley: Apocryphile Press.

Made in the USA
Las Vegas, NV
15 April 2023

70651800R00163